Fun for Friends

History

Trivia

Questions, answers & facts
to challenge your mind!

WS Publishing Group
www.WSPublishingGroup.com
San Diego, California

History Trivia

By Alex A. Lluch

Published by WS Publishing Group
San Diego, California
Copyright © 2013 by WS Publishing Group

For inquiries:
Log on to www.WSPublishingGroup.com
Email info@WSPublishingGroup.com

ISBN-13: 978-1-61351-036-0

Printed in China.

History Trivia

Congratulations! You've taken the first step to hours of fun – alone, or with your friends – answering the most fun and fascinating trivia questions about History. Whether you're a history aficionado or history challenged, this book is for you!

This entertaining book includes hundreds of questions based on common history knowledge, making it easy for most people to know the answers. However, it also includes details about popular events that will challenge any history buff. The best thing about this book: Every question includes highly compelling facts guaranteed to keep you reading for hours.

This book is the perfect companion for road trips, waiting in the DMV line, riding on the subway, or just hanging out at home. Keep this book on hand at work (for those much-needed breaks), in the bedroom (much better than watching reruns), in the bathroom (you might as well do something useful), in the kitchen (while waiting for the water to boil) or anywhere you find yourself with a few minutes to spare. You can even bring it on a first date to fill those awkward silences and keep the conversation flowing.

See an attractive person across the room but don't know how to approach him/her? Initiate the conversation with one of our captivating questions like, "What is broadly considered the world's best-selling toy of all time?" You will feel more confident with your new and improved knowledge, and everyone around you will want to get to know you better.

Friday night blues? Don't know what to do? Invite all your friends over and take turns picking categories and asking each other questions. Make it interesting by proposing fun rules such as: loser pays for drinks, winner gets a back massage, or anything else you can think of!

When you finish this book you will feel smarter, more informed … and maybe even thinner and taller. You'll be ready to test your new knowledge against your peers and show them how smart you are. You'll surely be the life of any party, as you'll never run out of interesting topics that make for good conversation.

So whether you loved or hated history during school, you will enjoy learning about the past in this friendly, fun and fact-filled book.

1. Adolf Hitler's first chosen profession was in which field?

   a) medicine
   b) art
   c) veterinary medicine
   d) architecture

2. Which European dictator did Harry Truman call a "little squirt?"

   a) Adolf Hitler
   b) Benito Mussolini
   c) Fidel Castro
   d) Joseph Stalin

3. Which despot destroyed his economy with a program called the "Great Leap Forward?"

   a) Pol Pot
   b) Mao Zedong
   c) Francisco Franco
   d) Benito Mussolini

4. In which city was Italian dictator Benito Mussolini's body displayed after his execution?

   a) Milan
   b) Rome
   c) Florence
   d) Stalingrad

5. The film *The Killing Fields* was set in Cambodia during the Khmer Rouge regime of:

   a) Mao Zedong
   b) Chiang Kai-shek
   c) Pol Pot
   d) Kim Jong Il

1. art

Historians have theorized that Hitler's political fanaticism only worsened after he was rejected from art school twice.

2. Joseph Stalin

He forbade his guards from entering his bedchamber. As a test he would occasionally scream in pain – guards who came into the room were duly executed.

3. Mao Zedong

He forced the people to give up farming to make steel. Locusts plagued what little food was left and millions starved.

4. Milan

Il Duce's body was stolen from its grave the following year and remained missing for several months.

5. Pol Pot

Under Pol Pot, money and religion were banned, school and healthcare were stopped, and parental authority was stripped.

1. Bubonic plague is just one of how many known types of plague?

   a) one type
   b) three types
   c) six types
   d) ten types

2. In 1900 an American let a mosquito carrying which disease bite him to prove how it spread?

   a) malaria
   b) Spanish flu
   c) tuberculosis
   d) yellow fever

3. Which is **not** one of the most common allergens?

   a) cockroaches
   b) pollen
   c) dust
   d) animal dander

4. Which matinee idol drew widespread attention to HIV/AIDS in 1985 after his diagnosis?

   a) Rock Hudson
   b) Cary Grant
   c) Gary Cooper
   d) Marlon Brando

5. What disease cut short the career of baseball legend Lou Gehrig?

   a) multiple sclerosis
   b) Parkinson's disease
   c) amyotrophic lateral sclerosis
   d) Huntington's disease

Diseases
Answers

1. three types

There's also pneumonic (5% chance of survival) and septicemic (dead in 14.5 hours). Bubonic is actually the least deadly.

2. yellow fever

Dr. Jesse William Lazear didn't tell anyone about his experiment; his colleagues figured it out after his death at age 34 in Cuba.

3. dust

Many things compose dust but most don't illicit reactions (like human skin). However, dust mites are known to prompt allergies.

4. Rock Hudson

Donations doubled after his diagnosis; within days of his death Congress approved $221 million for research.

5. amyotrophic lateral sclerosis

While bidding farewell to baseball on July 4, 1939 (with a career batting average of .340), he referred to his illness as a "bad break."

1. The day that the Stock Market *started* to crash in 1929 was called:
   - a) Black Friday
   - b) Black Wednesday
   - c) Black Thursday
   - d) Black Tuesday

2. Which president was shown in cartoons fighting a multi-headed National Bank "monster"?
   - a) Abraham Lincoln
   - b) Thomas Jefferson
   - c) Andrew Jackson
   - d) James K. Polk

3. Which presidential candidate gave the famed "Cross of Gold Speech" in 1896?
   - a) Theodore Roosevelt
   - b) William Jennings Bryan
   - c) Eugene V. Debs
   - d) Wendell Willkie

4. The largest bankruptcy in American history was declared by what financial firm?
   - a) Bank of America
   - b) Enron
   - c) WorldCom
   - d) Lehman Brothers

5. Which robber baron, named "the most hated man in America," escaped a murder attempt?
   - a) Henry Clay Frick
   - b) Andrew Carnegie
   - c) Charles M. Schwab
   - d) John D. Rockefeller

Economy
Answers

1. Black Thursday

Five days later on Black Tuesday, the Stock Market hit bottom as 16 million shares were sold— a one-day record that held for almost 40 years.

2. Andrew Jackson

He so loathed the institution that he told his V.P., "The bank is trying to kill me, but I will kill it!" And he did.

3. William Jennings Bryan

That year, he became the first candidate to campaign from a car. He unsuccessfully ran for president two more times.

4. Lehman Brothers

With $640 billion in assets gone, they were pegged as one of the parties at fault for the 2008 global economic crisis.

5. Henry Clay Frick

Shot three times and stabbed twice, he cheated death again by missing Titanic's maiden voyage, for which he had tickets.

1. Katharine Hepburn is remembered for her legendary romance with which leading man?

   a) Cary Grant
   b) Clark Gable
   c) Spencer Tracy
   d) Humphrey Bogart

2. Audrey Hepburn's most iconic style moments were the product of which famed designer's vision?

   a) Hubert de Givenchy
   b) Coco Chanel
   c) Christian Dior
   d) Yves Saint Laurent

3. Marilyn Monroe was married to baseball legend Joe DiMaggio then this acclaimed playwright:

   a) Neil Simon
   b) Tennessee Williams
   c) Arthur Miller
   d) Eugene O'Neill

4. Of Elizabeth Taylor's eight husbands, which one did she marry twice?

   a) Conrad Hilton
   b) Mike Todd
   c) Eddie Fischer
   d) Richard Burton

5. Which Hollywood hoofers made ten films and practically created the musical comedy genre?

   a) Gene Kelly & Leslie Caron
   b) Fred Astaire & Rita Hayworth
   c) Gene Kelly & Judy Garland
   d) Fred Astaire & Ginger Rogers

1. Spencer Tracy

Kate and Spence made nine films together during their 26-year relationship, including *Woman of the Year* and *Adam's Rib*.

2. Hubert de Givenchy

Their partnership was what Hollywood dreams are made of, he styled her for *Funny Face* and *Breakfast at Tiffany's*.

3. Arthur Miller

He wrote *The Misfits* for her; it was ultimately the last film she ever completed (it was Clark Gable's last, too).

4. Richard Burton

Even after their second divorce, friends used to catch the devoted pair holding hands under the table at dinner parties.

5. Fred Astaire & Ginger Rogers

Many women have since liked to note, "Ginger Rogers did everything Fred Astaire did except backwards and in high heels!"

1. Whose historic 1876 patent was filed an hour after Elisha Gray's applied for the same device?

   a) Thomas Edison
   b) Henry Ford
   c) Alexander Graham Bell
   d) George Westinghouse

2. Before his experiment with a kite and key, Ben Franklin invented which weather device?

   a) weathervane
   b) umbrella
   c) rain gutter
   d) lightning rod

3. Whose assistant died while trying to invent an electric tool that could trap souls?

   a) Philo T. Farnsworth
   b) Alexander Graham Bell
   c) Louis Daguerre
   d) Thomas Edison

4. The Wright Brothers made the first controlled, powered human flight possible in which state?

   a) Ohio
   b) California
   c) Kansas
   d) North Carolina

5. Which scientist wrote to FDR encouraging him to build an atom bomb before Hitler could?

   a) Albert Einstein
   b) Nikola Tesla
   c) Edwin Hubble
   d) Linus Pauling

1. **Alexander Graham Bell**

   Credited for inventing the telephone, Bell
   spent 30 years and $250,000 trying to make
   six-nippled sheep, believing two-nippled
   sheep were inefficient.

2. **lightning rod**

   Franklin was the first American celebrity.
   The French sold souvenirs with his face
   emblazoned on them on the streets of Paris.

3. **Thomas Edison**

   While it wasn't a ghostbuster box per se,
   he did hope to converse with departed
   personalities. The prototype was
   never revealed.

4. **North Carolina**

   Orville, who made the first flight, died mere
   months after Chuck Yeager's supersonic
   flight broke the sound barrier.

5. **Albert Einstein**

   After witnessing the destruction the bomb
   wrought, Einstein viewed his support for
   the program as one of his greatest mistakes.

1. The "Great Smog of '52" affected which city?

   a) London
   b) Houston
   c) San Francisco
   d) Dublin

2. Chernobyl was the first nuclear disaster to reach the highest threat level, which is:

   a) 1
   b) 5
   c) 7
   d) 10

3. What was the worst oil spill in history?

   a) Amoco Cadiz, 1978
   b) Exxon Valdez, 1989
   c) Kuwaiti oil fires, 1991
   d) Deepwater Horizon, 2010

4. Which town was made ill in the 1940s due to 21,000 tons of toxic waste unknowingly buried underneath it?

   a) Love Canal, NY
   b) Tonawanda, NY
   c) Three Mile Island, PA
   d) Wheeling, WV

5. On what river is Three Mile Island located?

   a) Allegheny
   b) Monongahela
   c) Ohio
   d) Susquehanna

1. London

Doctors later attributed 12,000 premature deaths to the air pollution that caused the four-day "pea souper."

2. 7

Scientists have stated that because of the disaster, the area around Chernobyl will not be safe to farm for 200 years.

3. Kuwaiti

Three of history's four worst spills took place during the Gulf War when Saddam Hussein began a scorched earth policy.

4. Love Canal, NY

Once the waste's presence became public knowledge, more than 90% of the families in Love Canal moved.

5. Susquehanna

The eyes of the U.S. turned toward the Susquehanna River in 1979 when a Three Mile Island nuclear reactor underwent a meltdown.

1. One of the most notorious man-eaters is Burundi's Gustave, who is what kind of creature?

a) lion
b) crocodile
c) tiger
d) wolf

2. Which river has caused more flooding deaths than any other river in the world?

a) Amazon River
b) Mississippi River
c) Nile River
d) Yellow River

3. Which two countries were gripped by the "Winter of Terror" in 1950-51?

a) Sweden & Norway
b) Germany & Poland
c) Austria & Switzerland
d) Holland & Belgium

4. The United States has suffered five of history's 10 most deadly:

a) blizzards
b) tornadoes
c) hurricanes
d) earthquakes

5. The Great Famine of 1845-52 caused a surge in U.S. immigrants from which country?

a) China
b) India
c) Ireland
d) Russia

1. **crocodile**

National Geographic has searched for the 20-foot-long, 2,000-lb. croc believed to have killed at least 200 people.

2. **Yellow River**

The three worst floods in history were all on China's Yellow River – combined, they claimed about 4.7 million lives.

3. **Austria & Switzerland**

That winter, 649 avalanches occurred in the Alps, resulting in 265 deaths and widespread property damage.

4. **blizzards**

1888 was the worst year for U.S. blizzards – 45 mph winds produced 50-ft. snowdrifts, making transportation impossible. The storm claimed over 400 lives.

5. **Ireland**

Called the "Potato Famine," massive potato crop loss starved one million people while another million moved to the U.S.

1. On May 31 and July 11 the Sun sets at the end of every numbered street in which city?

   a) Cairo
   b) Paris
   c) Athens
   d) New York City

2. What planet is the least explored planet in our Solar System?

   a) Pluto
   b) Mercury
   c) Neptune
   d) Uranus

3. Venus' atmosphere is full of clouds composed of which chemical that is toxic to humans?

   a) carbon monoxide
   b) nitrous dioxide
   c) sulfur dioxide
   d) helium monoxide

4. On what region of the Moon did the Apollo 11 crew land?

   a) Fra Mauro Highlands
   b) Sea of Tranquility
   c) Ocean of Storms
   d) Plain of Descartes

5. Much of Mars is covered by what?

   a) rust
   b) clay
   c) sand
   d) diamonds

1. **New York City**

   The event is called "Manhattanhenge" and was popularized by American astrophysicist Neil deGrasse Tyson.

2. **Mercury**

   Earth has only sent one spacecraft to Mercury — in 1974 NASA sent Mariner I to explore the hot, hot neighbor of the Sun.

3. **sulfur dioxide**

   Not only does it rain sulfuric acid, the atmospheric pressure is 92 times that of Earth, which would crush a person.

4. **Sea of Tranquility**

   Armstrong's first words upon landing: "Houston, Tranquility Base here. The *Eagle* has landed."

5. **rust**

   Mars is known as the "Red Planet" because of the considerable amount of fine, powdery rust, or iron oxide, that enrobes it.

1. The postage on incoming and outgoing mail was legally suspended for which president?

   a) Abraham Lincoln
   b) George Washington
   c) Thomas Jefferson
   d) Andrew Jackson

2. When the Library of Congress was burned by the British, which president restocked it?

   a) Thomas Jefferson
   b) James Madison
   c) James Monroe
   d) George Washington

3. Where did Andrew Jackson's nickname, "Old Hickory," come from?

   a) he owned a hickory farm
   b) his toughness
   c) he built things with hickory
   d) he cooked over hickory

4. How long did W.H. Harrison linger before dying from pneumonia he contracted at his inaugural?

   a) one week
   b) 31 days
   c) two months
   d) six months

5. Which president was taunted during his campaign about his illegitimate child?

   a) John F. Kennedy
   b) Thomas Jefferson
   c) Bill Clinton
   d) Grover Cleveland

1. George Washington

Congress created the law to demonstrate the nation's gratitude. Washington received so much mail he had to hire people to read it.

2. Thomas Jefferson

After the first was lost in the Burning of Washington Congress started a new collection with over 6,000 books from Thomas Jefferson's home.

3. his toughness

When people crossed him, which happened a lot, he beat them with his hickory cane; he even fought off an assassin with it.

4. 31 days

To show the people he wasn't too old, he gave a two-hour speech in cold weather without a coat, a move that inevitably killed him.

5. Grover Cleveland

The opposing party chanted "Ma, Ma, where's my Pa?" After he won, Cleveland's supporters responded: "Gone to the White House! Ha! Ha! Ha!"

1. The Redcoats that Washington ambushed when he crossed the Delaware were near which city?

   a) Boston
   b) Trenton, New Jersey
   c) Philadelphia
   d) Dover, Delaware

2. What site did Benedict Arnold plot to give to the British before his plan was discovered?

   a) Fort Ticonderoga
   b) Saratoga
   c) West Point
   d) Philadelphia

3. Who became the king of England at the end of the War of the Roses?

   a) Henry VII
   b) Henry VIII
   c) Richard III
   d) William the Conqueror

4. The Texian defenders of the Alamo were outnumbered by Santa Anna's Mexican army:

   a) 4 to 1
   b) 6 to 1
   c) 9 to 1
   d) 20 to 1

5. Where did the Civil War battle known as "the bloodiest day in American history" occur?

   a) Gettysburg
   b) Antietam
   c) Bull Run
   d) Chancellorsville

1. Trenton, New Jersey

He launched the Battle of Trenton on Christmas Night in 1776 knowing that the British Regulars would be busy celebrating.

2. West Point

Branded a "traitor" in American history, without his skilled leadership America may have lost early in the war.

3. Henry VII

Henry Tudor, a distant Lancaster relative, married Elizabeth of York and became Henry VII. Henry VIII was his son.

4. 9 to 1

The Alamo's defenders— Davy Crockett and James Bowie among them— fought for 13 days before Santa Anna's army laid siege.

5. Antietam

A soldier died every two seconds. Photos from Antietam were the first field photos of dead soldiers ever shown publicly.

1. When Idi Amin was overthrown in Uganda, he fled first to the country of which other autocrat?

   a) Omar al-Bashir
   b) Mobutu Sese Seko
   c) Muammar Gaddafi
   d) Saddam Hussein

2. Cuba's Fidel Castro, a longtime U.S. foe, is fanatical about which American sport?

   a) football
   b) basketball
   c) baseball
   d) Nascar

3. The body of which Bolshevik leader has been on public display since his death?

   a) Vladimir Lenin
   b) Joseph Stalin
   c) Nikita Khrushchev
   d) Leon Trotsky

4. Hitler said he would rather have "teeth pulled out" than deal with which man again?

   a) Benito Mussolini
   b) Hirohito
   c) Francisco Franco
   d) Joseph Stalin

5. Who was the only leader to successfully leave Stalin's Communist Cominform?

   a) Nicolae Ceausescu
   b) Leonid Brezhnev
   c) Enver Hoxha
   d) Josip Broz Tito

1. Muammar Gaddafi

Amin (erroneously) claimed to have defeated the British Empire and often wrote love letters to Queen Elizabeth II.

2. baseball

Cuba claims each president from Ike to Clinton tried to kill Castro at least 16 times (Nixon allegedly tried 184 times).

3. Vladimir Lenin

The odd look of his corpse (even for an embalmed body) leads many to suspect that some or all of the "body" is now wax.

4. Francisco Franco

Chevy Chase had a running gag on *SNL* where he would announce: "Generalissimo Francisco Franco is still dead."

5. Josip Broz Tito

Historians believe that the Yugoslavian statesman actually poisoned Stalin in order to permanently rid himself of his constant aggressor.

1. If the chickenpox virus is reactivated in someone's system, what illness will befall them?

a) tularemia
b) measles
c) shingles
d) mononucleosis

2. What is the only contagious disease to have been eliminated through vaccination?

a) polio
b) measles
c) scarlet fever
d) smallpox

3. Which illness was once known commonly as "consumption"?

a) tuberculosis
b) scarlet fever
c) cholera
d) influenza

4. What did Medieval plague doctors wear in order to protect themselves against sickness?

a) strands of garlic
b) potpourri sachet
c) a cross
d) beak-like mask

5. What president might have survived his assassination if he hadn't also had sepsis?

a) James Garfield
b) John F. Kennedy
c) Abraham Lincoln
d) William McKinley

Diseases
Answers

1. shingles

Chickenpox is merely a nuisance compared to the pain of shingles, which often affects only one side of a person's body.

2. smallpox

Smallpox wasn't always fatal. Elizabeth I survived it; Lincoln delivered the "Gettysburg Address" while infected.

3. tuberculosis

The 17,000-year killer has infected Andrew Jackson, 6 First Ladies, and authors Whitman, Thoreau, Keats and Orwell.

4. beak-like mask

The beak was stuffed with aromatic materials like rose petals and cloves. Doctors treated plague sufferers through bloodletting and placing frogs on their swollen lymph nodes.

5. James Garfield

Doctors reached into his wounds without washing their hands first, introducing the blood infection that killed him.

1. Who called Ronald Reagan's economic policy "voodoo economics"?

   a) George H. W. Bush
   b) Jimmy Carter
   c) Walter Mondale
   d) Bill Clinton

2. An outbreak of what type of influenza played a big role in the Panic of 1873?

   a) Spanish
   b) equine
   c) bovine
   d) Asian

3. In 1886 the U.S. economy tanked after the "Winter of Death," when which animal died off?

   a) buffalo
   b) chickens
   c) cows
   d) horses

4. The South's economy was all but completely consumed in 1919 by a plague of what insect?

   a) grasshopper
   b) boll weevil
   c) cicada
   d) locust

5. It has been claimed that in a bad economy sales of what product go up?

   a) canned food
   b) tires
   c) guns
   d) lipstick

1. **George H. W. Bush**

He was later made Reagan's V.P. to "unite" the Republican Party. They warmed their frosty relationship with a weekly Tex-Mex lunch.

2. **equine**

99% of U.S. horses were infected and coal could no longer be hauled to trains. As many as 20,000 businesses were ruined.

3. **cows**

Summertime overgrazing followed by a record cold spell killed half of the country's cattle, bankrupting an entire industry.

4. **boll weevil**

Enterprise, Alabama was so grateful for the lesson in agricultural diversification that they made a boll weevil monument.

5. **lipstick**

The head of Estée Lauder once said it's an affordable luxury that fills in for desired purchases during hard times.

1. The romantically involved costars of *To Have and Have Not* were known by these nicknames:
   a) Kate & Spence
   b) Liz & Dick
   c) Ma & Pa
   d) Bogie & Baby

2. Which screen star was born Archibald Leach and worked in a circus until he began acting?
   a) Clark Gable
   b) Humphrey Bogart
   c) Cary Grant
   d) James Dean

3. What did actor Paul Newman say he considered his greatest achievement?
   a) his family
   b) his Academy Award
   c) his philanthropic empire
   d) being on Nixon's Enemies List

4. For which film did Sidney Poitier win the first leading role Oscar awarded to a black man?
   a) *Guess Who's Coming to Dinner?*
   b) *Lilies of the Field*
   c) *In the Heat of the Night*
   d) *To Sir, with Love*

5. Who kept his Best Actor Academy Award in his father's hardware store in Pennsylvania?
   a) Tom Hanks
   b) Dustin Hoffman
   c) Jimmy Stewart
   d) Gregory Peck

1. Bogie & Baby

Despite their 25-year age difference, they were devoted to each other. They were married for 12 years, until his death.

2. Cary Grant

Despite his ranking as the American Film Institute's second greatest actor of all time, Grant never won an Academy Award.

3. being on Nixon's Enemies List

Though 576 people were on Tricky Dick's revised "master list," Newman was one of only 20 people on the original list.

4. *Lilies of the Field*

It was 38 years before another black actor claimed the trophy, when Denzel Washington won in 2001 for *Training Day*.

5. Jimmy Stewart

"Philadelphia" in *The Philadelphia Story* was spelled wrong on the statue. The role was originally offered to Spencer Tracy.

1. In what year was the first Internet link established?

   a) 1969
   b) 1979
   c) 1989
   d) 1999

2. American military personnel used Slinkys as radio antennae during which war?

   a) World War II
   b) Korean War
   c) Vietnam War
   d) Desert Storm

3. Henry Ford's most significant achievement was his 1913 invention of what?

   a) 9 to 5 workday
   b) traffic light
   c) moving assembly line
   d) labor union

4. The 1852 invention of which device made the later invention of skyscrapers possible?

   a) Bessemer steelmaking process
   b) motorized crane
   c) elevator
   d) indoor sprinkler systems

5. In what decade were Wonder Bread, aerosol cans and frozen foods first introduced?

   a) 1900s
   b) 1920s
   c) 1940s
   d) 1950s

1. **1969**

   It would take approximately one million human brains to retain all of the information that exists as of 2012 on the Internet.

2. **Vietnam War**

   The Slinky song is the longest-running jingle in history. A regular Slinky, if straightened, is 87 feet long.

3. **moving assembly line**

   Its efficiency lowered the Model T's retail price 65%. He also paid his workers three times the average factory salary.

4. **elevator**

   NYC was home to the world's tallest building for 79 years, though four different structures had the title in that time.

5. **1920s**

   The first popularly used aerosol product was "bug bomb," which American WWII soldiers used to ward off malaria-ridden mosquitos.

1. What part of the Exxon Valdez oil tanker was broken, leading to its 1989 spill?

   a) oil tanks
   b) engine pump
   c) radar
   d) brakes

2. In 1919 Boston suffered calamity when what spilled in the city?

   a) oil
   b) whiskey
   c) farm waste
   d) molasses

3. This notable astronaut was onboard when the Space Shuttle *Challenger* exploded in 1986:

   a) Sally Ride
   b) Gus Grissom
   c) Christa McAuliffe
   d) Alan Shepard

4. Which shipping company operated the RMS *Titanic*?

   a) Red Star Line
   b) Cunard Line
   c) White Star Line
   d) Black Ball Line

5. Where was Amelia Earhart destined when she disappeared in 1937?

   a) Howland Island
   b) San Francisco
   c) Honolulu
   d) Tokyo

Man-Made Disasters

Answers

1. radar

Without radar, the third mate was oblivious to the reef that they ultimately hit, spilling 55 million gallons of oil as a result.

2. molasses

A storage tank burst, letting loose a torrent of molasses that coursed through streets at 35 mph. 21 people were killed.

3. Christa McAuliffe

She was NASA's first "Teacher in Space," a fact that drew national attention. Her entire class was present at the launch.

4. White Star Line

Approximately 1,517 people died after the *Titanic* hit an iceberg. It was the fifth-worst maritime disaster in history.

5. Howland Island

It's still one of the greatest mysteries in history, though clues point to an emergency island landing, where she ultimately died.

Natural Disasters

1. In March 1925, the Tri-State Tornado left 625 people dead in Missouri, Illinois and:

   a) Indiana
   b) Kentucky
   c) Iowa
   d) Tennessee

2. Which disease is the deadliest one in human history?

   a) measles
   b) malaria
   c) tuberculosis
   d) smallpox

3. The deadliest hurricane to hit North America primarily struck which U.S. state?

   a) Florida
   b) Texas
   c) North Carolina
   d) Louisiana

4. In which year did California's most legendary earthquake rattle San Francisco?

   a) 1900
   b) 1904
   c) 1906
   d) 1912

5. In 1856, 4,000 people died when the Palace of the Grand Master in Rhodes was struck by what?

   a) lightning
   b) tornado
   c) hurricane
   d) mudslide

Natural Disasters

1. Indiana

The deadliest twister in U.S. history left a continuous path of damage that was a world-record length of 219 miles.

2. smallpox

From 1900 until its eradication in 1980, smallpox claimed an estimated 300 million lives.

3. Texas

The Galveston Hurricane of 1900 was the deadliest natural disaster in U.S. history, resulting in 6,000-12,000 deaths.

4. 1906

The earthquake and ensuing fires were the third worst natural disaster in U.S. history and worst California disaster overall.

5. lightning

Lightning struck the 450-yr-old palace, detonating the ammunition that was stored in the vault. The explosion completely obliterated the palace and church of St. John.

1. The largest planet in our Solar System was named for which Roman god?

   a) the god of war
   b) the god of the sea
   c) the king of the gods
   d) the god of the underworld

2. Saturn's many rings are primarily composed of what?

   a) ice particles
   b) nitrogen
   c) sand
   d) hydrogen

3. Which planet rotates at the most tilted angle?

   a) Neptune
   b) Mercury
   c) Jupiter
   d) Uranus

4. What is the name of Neptune's largest moon?

   a) Io
   b) Triton
   c) Galatea
   d) Callisto

5. When Pluto lost its planetary status, it was downgraded to what?

   a) planetoid
   b) moon of Neptune
   c) dead comet
   d) dwarf planet

Planets and Stars

Answers

1. **the king of the gods**

   Jupiter was the Roman equivalent of the Greeks' Zeus, who was also the god of lightning.

2. **ice particles**

   Though several planets in the Solar System have rings, Saturn's are the broadest, most colorful and prominent.

3. **Uranus**

   The tilt is so severe, the poles point toward the Sun, or what we would perceive on Earth as sideways instead of up and down.

4. **Triton**

   It's the only one of the 13 Neptunian moons that's spheroidal. It was likely a dwarf planet before becoming a moon.

5. **dwarf planet**

   People were upset and confused over the −390°F dwarf planet's reclassification, a fact that had been taught in school for 76 years.

1. Which president was arrested for vehicular homicide?

   a) Franklin Pierce
   b) Andrew Jackson
   c) Lyndon B. Johnson
   d) John F. Kennedy

2. Which of Abraham Lincoln's sons was the only one to live past the age of 18?

   a) Tad
   b) Willie
   c) Robert
   d) Edward

3. What president's alcoholism was largely a result of being away from his wife, who he adored?

   a) Franklin Pierce
   b) Theodore Roosevelt
   c) Ulysses S. Grant
   d) George W. Bush

4. Which president's wife was later known as "Lemonade Lucy"?

   a) Calvin Coolidge
   b) Herbert Hoover
   c) Rutherford B. Hayes
   d) Benjamin Harrison

5. George W. Bush and what other President both had Vice Presidents who shot men while in office?

   a) Franklin D. Roosevelt
   b) Abraham Lincoln
   c) Thomas Jefferson
   d) Andrew Jackson

1. Franklin Pierce

Pierce's buggy hit and killed a woman. The collision was later deemed unavoidable and the charges were dropped.

2. Robert

Robert Todd Lincoln was present at the assassinations of Presidents Garfield and McKinley.

3. Ulysses S. Grant

Julia had crossed eyes and was encouraged to fix them surgically, but Ulysses objected saying "he liked her that way."

4. Rutherford B. Hayes

A prohibitionist, she only served non-alcoholic drinks in the White House, though lemonade generally wasn't one of them.

5. Thomas Jefferson

Dick Cheney accidentally shot a friend in the face while hunting; Aaron Burr shot and killed Alexander Hamilton in a duel.

1. Which Confederate general had 30 horses shot out from under him during the Civil War?

   a) Robert E. Lee
   b) Nathan Bedford Forrest
   c) Stonewall Jackson
   d) J.E.B. Stuart

2. The infamous courtesan Mata Hari was a WWI spy for one (or both) of which two countries?

   a) Spain or France
   b) Italy or Germany
   c) France or Germany
   d) Germany or Spain

3. The Nazis borrowed the fight song of which American university for the "Sieg Heil" march?

   a) Yale
   b) Princeton
   c) Harvard
   d) Georgetown

4. The TV show *M*A*S*H* was set during which American war?

   a) Korean War
   b) Vietnam War
   c) World War II
   d) Balkan War

5. The Battles of Brandywine, Cowpens and Saratoga were all part of what war?

   a) French and Indian War
   b) Civil War
   c) Revolutionary War
   d) War of 1812

1. Nathan Bedford Forrest

He also killed 31 men in hand-to-hand combat, prompting his remark, "I was a horse ahead at the end."

2. France or Germany

The body of the accused double-agent was donated to science after her execution. In 2000 her head was declared missing.

3. Harvard

Hitler kept a framed photo of American industrialist Henry Ford on his desk, and Henry Ford kept one of him.

4. Korean War

The finale was a cultural touchstone— it remains the most watched episode in U.S. TV history with 125 million viewers.

5. Revolutionary War

Benedict Arnold was ordered to stay out of the second Saratoga, but his rallying of the troops likely secured their win.

1. *The Onion* duped a Chinese newspaper into believing _____ was *People*'s "Sexiest Man Alive."

   a) Bashar al-Assad
   b) Kim Jong-un
   c) Mao Zedong
   d) Chiang Kai-shek

2. Dictators are generally associated with what psychological affliction?

   a) obsessive compulsive disorder
   b) attention deficit disorder
   c) schizophrenia
   d) megalomania

3. What comedian mocked dictatorships— and one autocrat in particular— in *The Great Dictator*?

   a) Groucho Marx
   b) Mel Brooks
   c) Charlie Chaplin
   d) Woody Allen

4. Augusto Pinochet rose to power after what organization assassinated his predecessor?

   a) British Secret Service
   b) FBI
   c) Tijuana drug cartel
   d) CIA

5. The body of which dictator's wife went missing when he fled the country before her burial?

   a) Nicolae Ceausescu
   b) Idi Amin
   c) Juan Perónt
   d) Saddam Hussein

1. **Kim Jong-un**

   Not realizing that the title was a joke, the communist paper celebrated their North Korean leader with a 55-page photo spread.

2. **megalomania**

   Some of the associated qualities include: intolerance of criticism, grandiosity, narcissistic abuse, rage, and manipulation.

3. **Charlie Chaplin**

   He was inspired by the Nazi propaganda film, *Triumph of the Will*, which he found hilarious.

4. **CIA**

   Shortly after the coup d'état that put him in power, Pinochet had 3,197 of his opponents murdered.

5. **Juan Perón**

   Somehow her body ended up in Italy. Juan then had her moved to Spain, where he was hiding. After his death in 1974, she was buried a third time next to him in Argentina.

1. What disease did Columbus bring back from the New World that later spread through Europe?

a) smallpox
b) yellow fever
c) syphilis
d) plague

2. Beethoven's cause of death remains a mystery after scientists ruled out which poison?

a) arsenic
b) lead
c) salmonella
d) mercury

3. What characterized the mass psychogenic illness that shut down 14 African schools in 1962?

a) screaming
b) laughing
c) fainting
d) dancing

4. In 1518 France was besieged by a plague of what?

a) laughing
b) screaming
c) dancing
d) inexplicable suicides

5. What did a person likely eat if they are afflicted with trichinosis?

a) beef
b) pork
c) cheese
d) fruit

Diseases

1. syphilis

He's believed to have indirectly infected:
Henry VIII, Hitler, Napoleon, Nietzsche,
Van Gogh, Flaubert, Al Capone and,
fittingly, Casanova.

2. lead

New tests in 2010 determined the lead
content in his hair was normal. Hepatitis
and cirrhosis still remain possible factors
in his death.

3. laughing

For almost a year it affected 1,000 people
and resulted in rashes, crying, flatulence,
crying and fainting.

4. dancing

There's still no medical explanation for why
400 people danced nonstop, many to the
point of stroke and heart attack.

5. pork

It comes from eating undercooked pork.
Most larvae variants can survive freezing
and are only killed through heat.

1. As of 2012, which company's stock (the sum of all its shares) was the most valuable?

   a) Microsoft
   b) Apple
   c) Exxon Mobil
   d) Berkshire Hathaway

2. What is the largest denomination of currency ever printed by the United States?

   a) $10,000 bill
   b) $100,000 bill
   c) $1 million bill
   d) $10 million bill

3. In what state is Exxon Mobil, the largest company in the world by revenue, headquartered?

   a) Alaska
   b) Michigan
   c) Texas
   d) California

4. What was the average cost of a house in 1947?

   a) $3,000
   b) $13,000
   c) $23,000
   d) $33,000

5. The central character in which movie was a Nobel Laureate in Economics?

   a) *Wall Street*
   b) *Rain Man*
   c) *A Beautiful Mind*
   d) *Pi*

1. **Apple**

   In August Apple hit $665 billion, beating the previous all-time high set by Microsoft, who reached $618 billion in 1999.

2. **$100,000 bill**

   In 1934-35 the gold certificates featuring Woodrow Wilson were printed for treasury use only, not for the public.

3. **Texas**

   Seven of the world's top companies specialize in oil and gas, and three are U.S.-based: Chevron and ConocoPhillips.

4. **$13,000**

   Thanks to the G.I. Bill, returning soldiers and WWII veterans were able to afford homes, and "the suburbs" started springing up around the nation.

5. *A Beautiful Mind*

   The movie was released years before John Forbes Nash was awarded the 1994 Nobel Memorial Prize for game theory.

1. Joan Crawford, as portrayed in *Mommie Dearest*, absolutely loathed what object?

   a) panties
   b) bubblegum
   c) wire hangers
   d) hula hoops

2. Which future film icon got her start on stage singing with "The Gumm Sisters"?

   a) Judy Garland
   b) Shirley Temple
   c) Barbra Streisand
   d) Ginger Rogers

3. What film star is **not** known as a "method actor," the practice taught at the Actor's Studio?

   a) Daniel Day-Lewis
   b) Marlon Brando
   c) Morgan Freeman
   d) Christian Bale

4. What original "Blonde Bombshell" was godmother to mobster Bugsy Siegel's daughter?

   a) Marilyn Monroe
   b) Jean Harlow
   c) Mae West
   d) Carole Lombard

5. Which film icon will be depicted on Sweden's 50 Kronor banknote starting in 2015?

   a) Audrey Hepburn
   b) Ingrid Bergman
   c) Elizabeth Taylor
   d) Greta Garbo

Hollywood

1. wire hangers

Joan Crawford's real name is Lucille LeSueur, a name MGM studio did not particularly care for. As a publicity stunt, they held a contest where they let fans rename her.

2. Judy Garland

At almost the same time Garland passed away in London, a tornado struck Kansas.

3. Morgan Freeman

Actor's Studio alumni includes: Alec Baldwin, Robert De Niro, James Dean, Dustin Hoffman, Paul Newman and Marilyn Monroe.

4. Jean Harlow

She was the first actress to appear on the cover of *Life* magazine. She died at 26 from nephritis as a result of kidney failure.

5. Greta Garbo

She wouldn't give interviews or attend premieres during her career; she spent her later years secluded from the public.

1. What was the first surgical anesthetic used in the United States?

   a) ether
   b) chloroform
   c) nitrous oxide
   d) cocaine

2. Which heralded fashion designer stitched the first "little black dress"?

   a) Christian Dior
   b) Yves Saint Laurent
   c) Gianni Versace
   d) Coco Chanel

3. What scientist coined the term "radioactivity"?

   a) Albert Einstein
   b) Marie Curie
   c) Robert Oppenheimer
   d) Guglielmo Marconi

4. In the 1880s Thomas Edison was in an electric innovation "War of Currents" against:

   a) Alexander Graham Bell
   b) Alessandro Volta
   c) Nikola Tesla
   d) Alva Fisher

5. What guided missile inventor was hired by NASA to create the rocket that went to the Moon?

   a) Hermann von Helmholtz
   b) Chuck Yeager
   c) Carl Sagan
   d) Wernher von Braun

1. nitrous oxide

Dentist Horace Wells first used it in 1844. He later committed suicide after an addiction to chloroform drove him insane.

2. Coco Chanel

She showed her first "LBD" in a 1926 issue of *Vogue*; they called it "Chanel's Ford," comparing it to the simplicity of Ford's Model T.

3. Marie Curie

She's the only Nobel Laureate in multiple sciences. She was ultimately killed by the radioactivity she studied.

4. Nikola Tesla

Tesla's patents were controlled by George Westinghouse, Edison's real rival. Tesla was the archetypical "mad scientist."

5. Wernher von Braun

A pioneer of Nazi weapon technology during WWII, Braun later received U.S. amnesty by agreeing to design rockets for NASA.

1. What force was so intense during the
   Dust Bowl it caused wire fences to shoot
   blue flames?

   a) lightning
   b) heat
   c) wildfires
   d) static electricity

2. What American food tycoon booked a
   suite on the *Titanic* but canceled at the
   last minute?

   a) Joseph Campbell
   b) Milton Hershey
   c) Clarence Birdseye
   d) Oscar Mayer

3. The RMS *Lusitania* was an ocean liner
   belonging to what country?

   a) Germany
   b) United States
   c) Ireland
   d) Great Britain

4. What violent episode of the civil
   rights movement did **not** occur during
   JFK's presidency?

   a) Little Rock Nine
   b) murder of Medgar Evers
   c) Freedom Rides
   d) Ole Miss riot

5. The Haymarket riot occurred after a labor
   demonstration bombing in what city?

   a) Boston
   b) New York City
   c) Detroit
   d) Chicago

1. static electricity

Two people touching could produce a spark so powerful it would knock them down. People dragged chains on their cars to keep their cars grounded.

2. Milton Hershey

Millionaire John Jacob Astor was onboard and reportedly said, "I asked for ice, but this is ridiculous."

3. Great Britain

A WWI German U-boat sunk it, believing it secretly carried weapons. While Britain claimed it was just a passenger liner, later investigation found munitions aboard.

4. Little Rock Nine

Ike federalized troops in 1957 to get the nine students into Little Rock's Central High during the integration crisis.

5. Chicago

The Haymarket riot, for which eight anarchists were convicted, was the origin of worldwide May Day workers' holidays.

1. Which disease killed as many people in 2 years as the Black Death killed in 200?
   a) tuberculosis
   b) smallpox
   c) Spanish flu
   d) cholera

2. The fictive disease in *Outbreak* closely resembled which horrifying real-life contagion?
   a) bubonic plague
   b) tuberculosis
   c) Ebola
   d) cholera

3. What natural disaster hit Washington, D.C. while the British were burning it in the War of 1812?
   a) blizzard
   b) earthquake
   c) tornado
   d) flood

4. In 2007, a tornado wider than the city itself destroyed Greensburg, a city in what state?
   a) Kansas
   b) Missouri
   c) Iowa
   d) Oklahoma

5. All but one of the 10 deadliest natural disasters in history took place on what continent?
   a) Europe
   b) Africa
   c) South America
   d) Asia

1. Spanish flu

While the origination of the virus was most likely U.S. or France, it was so named for the intense media attention it received in Spain.

2. Ebola

Ebola looks like the flu, at first. Then, itchy bruises follow right before the afflicted dies from multiple organ failure.

3. tornado

As the White House and Capitol burned in 100°F heat, a hellacious storm set over the city and drove the British out.

4. Kansas

The EF5 tornado was more than one mile wide, completely destroying 95% of the city and killing 11 of the 1,500 Greensburg residents.

5. Asia

Asia has lost millions to a famine, a tsunami, two floods, two hurricanes and four earthquakes dating back to 526.

1. Which Catholic cleric was the first astronomer to prove the Earth revolves around the Sun?

   a) Galileo Galilei
   b) Nicolaus Copernicus
   c) Tycho Brahe
   d) Issac Newton

2. The Tunguska Event was a 1908 explosion in Siberia caused by what celestial object?

   a) meteoroid
   b) asteroid
   c) moon rock
   d) solar flare

3. What planet was discovered by German-born British astronomer William Herschel in 1781?

   a) Neptune
   b) Uranus
   c) Jupiter
   d) Venus

4. The ancient Romans called the morning view (or aspect) of what bright planet "Lucifer"?

   a) Mars
   b) Mercury
   c) Venus
   d) Jupiter

5. In 2012 scientists were surprised to discover water ice on what planet?

   a) Uranus
   b) Saturn
   c) Mars
   d) Mercury

Planets and Stars

1. Nicolaus Copernicus

He wouldn't let his work be publicly released until after his death so that he didn't have to face the Church's rebuke.

2. meteoroid

It exploded in the atmosphere and never hit the ground. A meteor must survive ground impact to be considered a meteorite.

3. Uranus

It's blanketed by a complex layered cloud system, with water-based clouds in the lower layers and methane clouds on top.

4. Venus

The name means "light-bringer." The evening aspect was known as "Vesper." The Greeks believed the varied views were actually two separate stars.

5. Mercury

Though the planet is very near the Sun, its poles are actually in permanent shadows, allowing water to stay frozen.

1. Which President could write in Latin with one hand while also writing in Greek with the other hand?

   a) Thomas Jefferson
   b) Bill Clinton
   c) James Garfield
   d) Abraham Lincoln

2. What was the first gift Grover Cleveland gave his future wife Frances?

   a) diamond locket
   b) wedding dress
   c) baby carriage
   d) Model T

3. Congress voted to give whose wife an honorary seat in Congress after his death?

   a) Abraham Lincoln
   b) John F. Kennedy
   c) Franklin D. Roosevelt
   d) James Madison

4. A Woodrow Wilson quote, celebrating the Ku Klux Klan, was used in what silent movie?

   a) *The Birth of a Nation*
   b) *The Jazz Singer*
   c) *The General*
   d) *Ziegfeld Follies*

5. Who was the last president to have facial hair while in office?

   a) Theodore Roosevelt
   b) Warren G. Harding
   c) William Howard Taft
   d) Gerald Ford

1. **James Garfield**

   Garfield, President for just six months, was exceptionally smart— he also devised a proof for the Pythagorean theorem.

2. **baby carriage**

   The gift celebrated her birth; she was the child of his law partner. They wed in the White House 21 years later.

3. **James Madison**

   Renowned for her enthralling parties, Dolley also introduced ice cream to the White House at the President's second inauguration. Her favorite flavor: oyster.

4. ***The Birth of a Nation***

   During his presidency, Wilson re-segregated Washington, D.C., a move that resulted in the demotion and termination of many African-American federal employees.

5. **William Howard Taft**

   The last mustachioed candidate was Thomas Dewey in 1948. Lincoln was the first bearded President.

1. People who evaded the Vietnam Draft were pardoned by which president?

a) Gerald Ford
b) Ronald Reagan
c) Jimmy Carter
d) Bill Clinton

2. Which famed American general's home became Arlington National Cemetery?

a) George Washington
b) George S. Patton
c) Benedict Arnold
d) Robert E. Lee

3. Which Union general burned his way through Georgia, notably Atlanta, during the Civil War?

a) William Tecumseh Sherman
b) Ulysses S. Grant
c) George McClellan
d) George Meade

4. Which Hollywood bombshell was the most popular American pinup during World War II?

a) Marilyn Monroe
b) Betty Grable
c) Rita Hayworth
d) Jayne Mansfield

5. Which Hollywood star didn't take time away from his film career to serve in World War II?

a) Jimmy Stewart
b) Audie Murphy
c) Cary Grant
d) Mel Brooks

1. Jimmy Carter

Muhammad Ali was the most notable conscientious objector— he avoided jail but was stripped of his heavyweight title.

2. Robert E. Lee

The Union seized his property as punishment for his role in the war and turned his front yard into a cemetery.

3. William Tecumseh Sherman

"Sherman's March to the Sea" was part of a "scorched earth" strategy. He left about $100 million in damage in his wake.

4. Betty Grable

A photo of her in a white bathing suit— the iconic pinup— was one of *Life*'s "100 Photos that Changed the World."

5. Cary Grant

He gave his wartime pay to the war effort and secretly served as a British Intelligence agent, watching for possible Nazi sympathizers.

1. What African despot was stripped of an honorary knighthood by Queen Elizabeth II?

   a) Muammar Gaddafi
   b) Hosni Mubarak
   c) Robert Mugabe
   d) Idi Amin

2. Which African dictator was known for his leopard-skin hats?

   a) Mobutu Sese Seko
   b) Idi Amin
   c) Omar al-Bashir
   d) Hosni Mubarak

3. What dictator, kidnapped by pirates, demanded that they increase their ransom request?

   a) Saddam Hussein
   b) Muammar Gaddafi
   c) Julius Caesar
   d) Joseph Stalin

4. Saddam Hussein donated 27 liters of *what* fluid as "ink" for a handwritten Qur'an?

   a) gold
   b) his blood
   c) snake venom
   d) eagle blood

5. Which Soviet dictator was awarded the Nobel Peace Prize?

   a) Joseph Stalin
   b) Konstantin Chernenko
   c) Vladimir Lenin
   d) Mikhail Gorbachev

Dictators
Answers

1. Robert Mugabe

He was also stripped of titles from the Government of Jamaica, the Hunger Project, and honorary degrees from three universities.

2. Mobutu Sese Seko

He ordered that all news broadcasts had to begin with an image of him descending from the clouds.

3. Julius Caesar

He scoffed at their initial ransom of 1,140 lbs. of silver and insisted they double it. He returned later with a fleet and cut each pirate's throat.

4. his blood

He insisted all political officers read his 19-volume biography. He liked to wear a cowboy hat (a gift from Fidel Castro) while watching torture videos.

5. Mikhail Gorbachev

He introduced glasnost, or new freedoms to the people, in attempt to reform the Communist nation. His contributions helped end the Cold War.

1. Which disease would a pirate have been most likely to get?

a) scurvy
b) rickets
c) hepatitis
d) scabies

2. Who introduced the polio vaccine in 1955?

a) Edgar Crookshank
b) Louis Pasteur
c) Jonas Salk
d) Edward Jenner

3. Louis Pasteur developed the first vaccines for rabies and:

a) smallpox
b) rubella
c) anthrax
d) scarlet fever

4. If a "zombie apocalypse" ever occurs, the undead will come looking for what food?

a) human blood
b) human flesh
c) human brains
d) human hearts

5. W.C. Fields, Billie Holiday and Jack Kerouac all died from an addiction to what?

a) heroin
b) alcohol
c) opium
d) food

1. scurvy

In 1864, Ulysses S. Grant had vitamin-C enriched cranberries served to his army on Thanksgiving to help thwart the disease.

2. Jonas Salk

Salk gave the vaccine away for free because he felt he shouldn't profit from something that would benefit mankind.

3. anthrax

He is often best-remembered for the process he developed to treat milk and wine, which was aptly named after him: pasteurization.

4. human brains

In 2011 the CDC began training for a zombie apocalypse, noting (jokingly) it effectively prepared them for all hazards.

5. alcohol

It also led to the deaths of Truman Capote, F. Scott Fitzgerald, Mickey Mantle, Joseph McCarthy and Franklin Pierce.

1. How much did the cost of the Model T drop after the advent of Ford's moving assembly line?

   a) 33%
   b) 50%
   c) 70%
   d) 90%

2. What presidential candidate was deemed "out of touch" when a checkout scanner amazed him?

   a) Michael Dukakis
   b) Jimmy Carter
   c) George H. W. Bush
   d) Richard Nixon

3. Which company has the most employees?

   a) Wal-Mart
   b) IBM
   c) McDonald's
   d) Target

4. Which state produces the most apples?

   a) New York
   b) Pennsylvania
   c) California
   d) Washington

5. What makes the annual collection of federal income tax a legal right of the government?

   a) 16th Amendment, Constitution
   b) Article III, Constitution
   c) executive order, Pres. Wilson
   d) there's no law requiring taxes

Economy

1. **70%**

In 1909 a Model T cost $850. The 1913 creation of the moving line ultimately lowered it to $260 in the early '20s.

2. **George H. W. Bush**

Bush's scanner shock in 1992 implied he hadn't been in a supermarket since at least '74, when scanners came into use.

3. **Wal-Mart**

Wal-Mart has more than five times as many employees (2.2 million) as the second-biggest employer, IBM (433,362).

4. **Washington**

WA yields 60% of the third most valuable U.S. fruit crop. Apples are one of the only fruits grown in every state.

5. **16th Amendment, Constitution**

Prior to 1913 it was only collected off-and-on after Lincoln levied the first income tax in 1861 to pay for the Civil War.

1. What kind of car was James Dean driving during his fatal crash in 1955?

a) Ford Mustang
b) Austin-Healey Sprite
c) Porsche Spyder
d) Chevrolet Corvette

2. Richard Nixon ironically appointed what rock star to the Bureau of Narcotics and Dangerous Drugs?

a) Bob Dylan
b) Keith Richards
c) John Lennon
d) Elvis Presley

3. Which guitarist nearly became a Beatle when George Harrison briefly quit the band in 1969?

a) Keith Richards
b) Eric Clapton
c) Jimmy Page
d) Duane Allman

4. Where did choir boys turned rock stars Mick Jagger and Keith Richards meet?

a) on a train
b) at school
c) at a church event
d) at an underground blues show

5. Which personal hero did a 19-year-old Bob Dylan periodically visit in a psychiatric hospital?

a) Jack Kerouac
b) Pete Seeger
c) Elvis Presley
d) Woody Guthrie

1. **Porsche Spyder**

Decades later, specialists proved he wasn't speeding when he crashed, though he *was* ticketed for speeding just hours before.

2. **Elvis Presley**

Elvis hated drugs, stating prescriptions were not actually "drugs." Ironically, experts believe his premature heart attack was a result of long-term medication use.

3. **Eric Clapton**

He never took George's Beatles post but he did take his wife. Clapton married Patti Boyd Harrison in 1979.

4. **on a train**

Keith noticed the blues records Mick was carrying, which sparked a conversation and one of rock's greatest pairings.

5. **Woody Guthrie**

Dylan's "Song to Woody" was written for one of their many visits, later making its way onto his debut album.

1. The code name for the Manhattan Project's first nuclear test was what?

   a) Trinity
   b) Fat Man
   c) Oakridge
   d) Holy

2. Who founded a prestigious award program out of guilt for inventing dynamite?

   a) Joseph Pulitzer
   b) Alfred Nobel
   c) Enrico Fermi
   d) Nikola Tesla

3. Of which modern device did Leonardo da Vinci **not** craft a similar design?

   a) helicopter
   b) hydraulic pump
   c) elevator
   d) underwater breathing apparatus

4. Who helped devised a telegraphic "language" after inventing the electric telegraph?

   a) Thomas Edison
   b) Alexander Graham Bell
   c) Samuel Morse
   d) Benjamin Franklin

5. In what decade were aspirin, Jello-O, the radio and electric toaster introduced?

   a) 1860s
   b) 1870s
   c) 1890s
   d) 1910s

1. **Trinity**

   While watching the atomic bomb test, Robert Oppenheimer recalled the Bhagavad Gita line: "Now I am become Death, the destroyer of worlds."

2. **Alfred Nobel**

   After learning he was called "the merchant of death," he decided he wanted to be remembered for creating something good.

3. **elevator**

   Da Vinci was the first person to explain that the sky is blue because of how the atmosphere causes light particles to scatter.

4. **Samuel Morse**

   Before inventing the telegraph and Morse Code, he was a renowned portrait artist who painted the hall of Congress.

5. **1890s**

   The first toaster was called the Eclipse, and was made with iron wires that melted easily and posed huge fire hazards.

Man-Made Disasters
Questions

1. What noted abolitionist was behind (and ultimately hanged for) the Harper's Ferry Raid?

   a) Henry Ward Beecher
   b) John C. Fremont
   c) John Brown
   d) Frederick Douglass

2. Which rock and roll pioneer was **not** killed in the plane crash the "day the music died"?

   a) Ritchie Valens
   b) Buddy Holly
   c) Jerry Lee Lewis
   d) the "Big Bopper"

3. What was the central issue in the deadly 19th century conflict known as "Bleeding Kansas"?

   a) slavery
   b) newly discovered gold
   c) land rush ownership claims
   d) Indian removal

4. What were Kent State students protesting when National Guardsmen opened fire in 1970?

   a) My Lai Massacre
   b) Watergate-related crimes
   C) Fall of Saigon
   d) invasion of Cambodia

5. Who was the lawyer for the British soldiers criminally charged in the Boston Massacre?

   a) Samuel Adams
   b) Benjamin Franklin
   c) John Adams
   d) Thomas Jefferson

1. John Brown

He asked Harriet Tubman and Douglass to take part in the intended revolt, but she was ill and Douglass thought the plan would fail.

2. Jerry Lee Lewis

The "Big Bopper" took what was originally intended to be Waylon Jennings' seat. Singer Dion DiMucci was also supposed to be onboard, but backed out at the last minute.

3. slavery

Kansas got to vote on being a "free" or "slave" state, prompting seven years of violence and 50-100 deaths.

4. invasion of Cambodia

The kneeling girl in the Pulitzer Prize-winning photo of the event was a 14-year-old runaway, not a Kent State student.

5. John Adams

He took the case not because he believed them innocent, but because he wanted to ensure a fair trial. Of the eight tried, six were acquitted.

1. The deadliest heat wave in U.S. history took place in what year?

    a) 1978
    b) 1988
    c) 1998
    d) 2008

2. Limnic eruptions occur in what natural feature?

    a) geyser
    b) volcano
    c) lake
    d) steam vent

3. The worst eruption ever recorded, which led to the worst famine of the 1800s, occurred in:

    a) the Philippines
    b) Hawaii
    c) Italy
    d) Indonesia

4. Founding Father Thomas Lynch Jr. vanished at sea three years after signing what charter?

    a) Federalist Papers
    b) Articles of Confederation
    c) U.S. Constitution
    d) Declaration of Independence

5. The majority of "man-eating" deaths are committed by creatures in what taxonomic family?

    a) Felidae (feline)
    b) Canidae (canine)
    c) Crocodyloidea
    d) Lamnidae (white sharks)

1. **1988**

   Until Hurricane Katrina hit in 2005, the 1988-89 drought was the costliest natural disaster in U.S. history ($60 billion).

2. **lake**

   Also known as lake overturn, this type of disaster releases suffocating clouds of carbon dioxide. A 1986 limnic eruption in Cameroon asphyxiated 1,700 people.

3. **Indonesia**

   Mount Tambora killed 71,000 then set off "the last great subsistence crisis in the Western world."

4. **Declaration of Independence**

   Aaron Burr's daughter Theodosia, the most educated woman of her day, also vanished at sea. Myths of piracy abounded.

5. **Felidae (feline)**

   The most aggressive man-eaters have been tigers, leopards and lions, though crocs and wolves have had their fair share.

1. Which of the inner planets in our Solar System is the densest?

a) Earth
b) Venus
c) Mars
d) Mercury

2. A planet in the constellation of Cancer is made of what precious resource?

a) platinum
b) gold
c) diamond
d) sapphire

3. Which planet has winds that rage at speeds up to 1,300 miles per hour?

a) Mercury
b) Earth
c) Mars
d) Neptune

4. How often does Halley's comet pass by Earth?

a) every 26 years
b) every 76 years
c) every 186 years
d) every 256 years

5. After Jupiter, what is the largest planet in our Solar System?

a) Saturn
b) Uranus
c) Neptune
d) Earth

Planets and Stars
Answers

1. Earth

It's the densest of all the planets even though it is only the fifth-largest. However, it is the largest terrestrial planet.

2. diamond

It's twice as wide as Earth and would be worth $26.9 nonillion— whereas one million has six zeroes, one nonillion has 30.

3. Neptune

Its weather systems are so active that they're visible from space. Neptune has the strongest sustained winds in the Solar System.

4. every 76 years

It's the only short-period comet with naked-eye visibility. In 1986 it became the first comet viewed from a spacecraft.

5. Saturn

It also has the Solar System's second-largest moon: Titan. Larger than Mercury, it's the only moon with an atmosphere.

1. What was the familial relationship between Franklin and Eleanor Roosevelt before they wed?

   a) first cousins
   b) second cousins
   c) third cousins, twice removed
   d) fifth cousins, once removed

2. Of what baseball franchise was George W. Bush part-owner prior to becoming President?

   a) Houston Astros
   b) Texas Rangers
   c) New York Yankees
   d) Los Angeles Dodgers

3. Who successfully answered three My Little Pony questions on a radio quiz show?

   a) Ronald Reagan
   b) Bill Clinton
   c) Barack Obama
   d) George W. Bush

4. Which vegetable did George H. W. Bush notoriously despise?

   a) Brussels sprouts
   b) broccoli
   c) cabbage
   d) carrots

5. Who survived being shot during his presidency?

   a) Ronald Reagan
   b) James Monroe
   c) Andrew Jackson
   d) Theodore Roosevelt

1. **fifth cousins, once removed**

Their great-great-great-grandfathers were brothers. She was much more closely related to Theodore Roosevelt, who was her uncle.

2. **Texas Rangers**

The first President Bush met Babe Ruth in 1946 when he led the Yale baseball team in the College World Series.

3. **Bill Clinton**

His near-eidetic memory is well chronicled— he wowed heads of state by recalling street names in their capital cities.

4. **broccoli**

He famously vomited broccoli on the Prime Minister of Japan while battling the flu in 1992. He declared he'd never eat it again.

5. **Ronald Reagan**

Andrew Jackson was shot in the chest during a duel. The bullet was too close to his heart and could not be removed. He was elected President 23 years later.

1. What once-derided monument was the 10th favorite U.S. structure according to a 2007 poll?

   a) Tomb of the Unknowns
   b) WWII Memorial
   c) National Cemetery
   d) Vietnam Veterans Memorial

2. The "fugos" Japan sent toward the United States in World War II were what type of craft?

   a) airplanes
   b) balloons
   c) boats
   d) submarines

3. What nation received Germany's Zimmerman Telegram, which drew the United States into WWI?

   a) Japan
   b) England
   c) Austria
   d) Mexico

4. What kind of birds were placed on the Eiffel Tower during WWI to warn of enemy planes?

   a) eagles
   b) parrots
   c) starlings
   d) owls

5. The Battle of the Sink Hole in Missouri Territory was the last land battle of what war?

   a) Civil War
   b) Revolutionary War
   c) War of 1812
   d) French and Indian War

1. Vietnam Veterans Memorial

Over the years, the stark "Wall" bearing 58,272 names has come to be seen as a deeply personal, national treasure.

2. balloons

They were fire devices affixed to hydrogen balloons that road the jet stream from Japan – some made it as far as Texas.

3. Mexico

Germany offered to aid Mexico if they'd declare war on the United States. Enraged, America declared war on Germany.

4. parrots

They could hear planes before humans would. Field geese in Belgium and France similarly warned of impending WWI attacks.

5. War of 1812

Though the Battle of New Orleans famously occurred after the war's official end, Sink Hole took place four months later.

1. Many South Koreans believed what "dear leader" could control the weather with his moods?

   a) Mao Zedong
   b) Kim Jong-il
   c) Pol Pot
   d) Hirohito

2. What parliamentary politician counted Fidel Castro and Jimmy Carter among his pallbearers?

   a) Winston Churchill
   b) Golda Meir
   c) John Major
   d) Pierre Trudeau

3. Whose crumpled body was shown on T.V. to assure the Romanian people of his execution?

   a) Joseph Stalin
   b) Nicolae Ceausescu
   c) Adolf Hitler
   d) Josip Broz Tito

4. What maniacal 16th-century leader killed his own son and heir?

   a) Henry VIII
   b) Napoleon
   c) Genghis Khan
   d) Ivan the Terrible

5. The Ayatollah offered heaven and a bounty for the head of what *Satanic Verses* author?

   a) Christopher Hitchens
   b) Jerry Falwell
   c) Salman Rushdie
   d) Winston Churchill

Dictators
Answers

1. Kim Jong-il

He also claimed he invented hamburgers and is a naturally gifted golf savant, scoring 38-under-par on his first attempt at the game.

2. Pierre Trudeau

In 1974, a NY mobster claimed he was hired to kill Trudeau in hopes his funeral would draw Fidel Castro so he could kill him too.

3. Nicolae Ceausescu

After the executions of Ceausescu and his wife, news flashes in Bucharest declared, "The anti-Christ is dead!"

4. Ivan the Terrible

The act was accidental – in a rage he beat his son for defending his pregnant wife, who Ivan felt was dressed inappropriately.

5. Salman Rushdie

Rushdie still receives a "valentine" from Iran each February 14, reminding him they want to see him dead.

1. What did the extraterrestrial disease in *The Andromeda Strain* cause in victims?

   a) hemorrhaging
   b) blood clots
   c) liquified internal organs
   d) closed respiratory system

2. What ailment did Bob Dole, Rafael Palmiero and Pelé become identified with via T.V. ads?

   a) erectile dysfunction
   b) enlarged prostates
   c) macular degeneration
   d) insomnia

3. What herb was called "Russian Penicillin" because the Red Army used it medicinally?

   a) parsley
   b) basil
   c) rosemary
   d) garlic

4. In 1906 the first meningitis antiserum was produced in what common farm animal?

   a) cow
   b) horse
   c) pig
   d) chicken

5. What disease routinely ruined treks along the simulated Oregon Trail game?

   a) dysentery
   b) mad deer disease
   c) malaria
   d) scarlet fever

Diseases

Answers

1. blood clots

The crafty microbe rapidly mutates throughout the story, thriving in human blood. The book was credited with portraying "hideously plausible suspense."

2. erectile dysfunction

The drug they all pitched, Viagra, was originally created to treat angina and symptoms of heart disease.

3. garlic

The Egyptians, Greeks, Chinese and Cherokee all believed in its healing powers. The Red Army used it in WWI & WWII to prevent gangrene.

4. horse

Once called "brain fever," meningitis was highly fatal until antiserums were found; the mortality rate was about 90%.

5. dysentery

It's also a leading killer in war zones. There's still no vaccine and new strains have increasing antibiotic resistance.

1. As of 2012, which stock was the most expensive, per share?

   a) Berkshire Hathaway
   b) Google
   c) priceline.com
   d) Apple

2. According to legend, which historical figure gained fame for her unique protest against taxes?

   a) Mary Magdalene
   b) Joan of Arc
   c) Lady Godiva
   d) Marie Antoinette

3. Who is the top-grossing film star of all time, earning over $4 billion at the box office?

   a) Daniel Radcliffe
   b) Tom Hanks
   c) Harrison Ford
   d) Tom Cruise

4. Where did the "49ers" rush when gold was discovered in 1849?

   a) Donner Pass
   b) Yasgur's Farm
   c) Sleepy Hollow
   d) Sutter's Mill

5. Which state has no individual income tax?

   a) Colorado
   b) Mississippi
   c) Illinois
   d) Texas

1. Berkshire Hathaway

One share in Warren Buffett's company cost $121,049 in March 2012. Fourth-ranked priceline.com only traded at $655.

2. Lady Godiva

The name "Peeping Tom" was inspired by the man who reportedly lost his sight upon seeing the 11th century woman's nude protest horse ride.

3. Tom Hanks

As of 2012, 17 of his films have earned over $100 million. His top earners: the *Toy Story* trilogy and *Forrest Gump*.

4. Sutter's Mill

While the California Gold Rush is the best-remembered dash for riches, Alaska's 1896 Klondike Gold Rush attracted over 100,000 prospectors.

5. Texas

Alaska, Florida, Nevada, New Hampshire, South Dakota, Tennessee, Washington and Wyoming also forsake that revenue.

1. Who was **not** one of *SNL's* original "Not Ready for Prime Time Players"?

   a) Bill Murray
   b) Chevy Chase
   c) Gilda Radner
   d) Dan Aykroyd

2. Comedian George Carlin was arrested for performing a show about how many "Dirty Words"?

   a) "Five"
   b) "Seven"
   c) "Ten"
   d) "A Dozen"

3. Every actor who's worked in Hollywood is allegedly just "six degrees" of association from:

   a) Tom Cruise
   b) Robert De Niro
   c) Kevin Bacon
   d) Tom Hanks

4. Who was the original "head" of the "Rat Pack" before Sinatra became its iconic lead man?

   a) Marlon Brando
   b) Humphrey Bogart
   c) James Dean
   d) Cary Grant

5. Which movie is not considered a "Brat Pack" movie?

   a) *The Breakfast Club*
   b) *Sixteen Candles*
   c) *Ferris Bueller's Day Off*
   d) *St. Elmo's Fire*

Hollywood

1. Bill Murray

Chase left shortly after the beginning of the second season and was replaced by Murray a couple months later.

2. "Seven"

He was arrested on obscenity charges and the show's television broadcast resulted in a U.S. Supreme Court case.

3. Kevin Bacon

Cruise (*A Few Good Men*), De Niro (*Sleepers*) and Hanks (*Apollo 13*) are one degree from Bacon, having co-starred with him.

4. Humphrey Bogart

It was originally the "Clan" and involved various actors before evolving into its Sinatra, Martin, Davis and Lawford roster.

5. *Ferris Bueller's Day Off*

Brat Pack members include: Molly Ringwald, Emilio Estevez, Anthony Michael Hall, Rob Lowe, Andrew McCarthy, Ally Sheedy and Judd Nelson.

1. What appliance was invented with WWII radar technology and originally called "Radarange"?

   a) television
   b) radio
   c) cellular telephone
   d) microwave oven

2. Through what document was the Electoral College invented to elect the President?

   a) Declaration of Independence
   b) Constitution
   c) Bill of Rights
   d) Articles of Confederation

3. What early-Hollywood film comedian received a patent for a cardiac pulse rate monitor?

   a) Zeppo Marx
   b) Charlie Chaplin
   c) Bud Abbott
   d) Buster Keaton

4. In what state were the can opener, cotton gin, Colt .45 Revolver and Frisbee invented?

   a) Colorado
   b) Texas
   c) Connecticut
   d) North Carolina

5. In which war was the United States engaged when G.I. Joe first saw playroom action?

   a) Korean War
   b) World War II
   c) World War I
   d) Vietnam War

Inventions

1. microwave oven

The first food deliberately cooked in a microwave oven was popcorn; the second was an egg, which exploded.

2. Constitution

Article II, Section I established that electors would act as the intermediary between the people and the presidency.

3. Zeppo Marx

His second career as an engineer was his most financially profitable – his engineering works made him a multi-millionaire.

4. Connecticut

Canned food existed for 50 years before a tool was made to open the can. The original cans were so thick they had to be hammered open.

5. Vietnam War

The original 1963 prototype for G.I. Joe (which was released in 1964) sold on eBay in 2003 for $200,000.

1. What was the name of the plane that dropped the atomic bomb on Hiroshima?

a) *Enola Gay*
b) *Bockscar*
c) *Electra*
d) *My Gal Sal*

2. What legendary mob boss was involved in the 1929 St. Valentine's Day Massacre?

a) Carlo Gambino
b) Bugsy Siegel
c) Al Capone
d) Lucky Luciano

3. In 2009, the American Society of Civil Engineers gave America's infrastructure what grade?

a) "B-"
b) "C+"
c) "D"
d) "F"

4. What event caused a human stampede that resulted in 1,389 deaths?

a) World Cup qualifying match
b) Brooklyn Theater fire
c) Russian Emperor coronation
d) Michael Jackson concert in Germany

5. What African nation was responsible for the Lockerbie bombing of Pan Am Flight 103?

a) Libya
b) Zimbabwe
c) Uganda
d) Congo

1. *Enola Gay*

Of its 12-man crew, only three knew the total nature of their mission. The plane, Bockscar, dropped the bomb on Nagasaki 3 days later.

2. Al Capone

He targeted rival boss Bugs Moran but only got seven of his men. While he avoided charges, he was later jailed for tax evasion.

3. "D"

They projected it would take a five-year investment of $2.2 trillion to repair all of the structural failings.

4. Russian Emperor coronation

Thousands of people gathered, eager for tsar's gifts of food. They surged forward when a rumor circulated that there wasn't enough beer and pretzels for everyone.

5. Libya

All 259 onboard and 11 bystanders were killed in the 1988 bombing. Libya didn't take responsibility until 2003.

1. More than 25% of men in the Philippines' Aeta tribe have survived unprovoked attacks by:

   a) boa constrictors
   b) Komodo dragons
   c) reticulated pythons
   d) saltwater crocodiles

2. What landmass was a peninsula until floods made it an island 180,000-450,000 years ago?

   a) Hawaii
   b) Australia
   c) Sicily
   d) Great Britain

3. In what disaster scenario do people fill their bathtubs with water for drinking?

   a) earthquake
   b) tornado
   c) flood
   d) wildfire

4. In 1875, history's largest insect plague occurred when which pest invaded North America?

   a) killer bee
   b) termite
   c) locust
   d) moth

5. Operation Eagle Claw to rescue the Iranian hostages was impeded by what kind of event?

   a) earthquake
   b) tornado
   c) plague of locusts
   d) sandstorm

1. reticulated pythons

The forest-dwelling tribesmen and the pythons compete for the same prey: deer, pigs and monkeys.

2. Great Britain

One of history's greatest megafloods, loosing one million cubic meters of water per second, created the English Channel.

3. flood

Floods (from hurricanes or otherwise) contaminate water supplies, making a bathtub of clean water a valuable resource.

4. locust

The swarm was 1,800 by 110 miles wide and destroyed crops, wheat fields, laundry and fence posts. The skies were pitch black when they gathered.

5. sandstorm

Sand blanketed the runways, impeding helicopters. Many believe the mission's epic failure cost Jimmy Carter his re-election.

1. What was the last Apollo mission to the Moon?

   a) Apollo 13
   b) Apollo 15
   c) Apollo 17
   d) Apollo 19

2. Who was the youngest American to go into space?

   a) Gordon Cooper
   b) John Glenn
   c) Sally Ride
   d) Jim Lovell

3. Who was the first woman in space?

   a) Sally Ride
   b) Valentina Tereshkova
   c) Svetlana Savitskaya
   d) Mae Jemison

4. Which planet is furthest from the Sun?

   a) Neptune
   b) Uranus
   c) Pluto
   d) Saturn

5. Which Gemini astronaut was the first American to make a spacewalk?

   a) Frank Borman
   b) Jim Lovell
   c) Ed White
   d) Roger Chaffee

1. **Apollo 17**

   Apollo 17's Eugene Cernan and Jack Schmitt were the last of twelve asronauts to walk on the Moon.

2. **Sally Ride**

   She was 32 when she flew in 1983. She was also the first U.S. woman to go, 20 years after Soviet Valentina Tereshkova.

3. **Valentina Tereshkova**

   She flew into space in 1963. It was 19 years before the second woman, Savitskaya (also a Soviet) flew. American Sally Ride flew in '83.

4. **Neptune**

   With Pluto's demotion to dwarf planet, Neptune is officially the most distant from the Sun. It was discovered in 1846.

5. **Ed White**

   He was one of the three astronauts lost in a fire during Apollo 1 tests, along with Project Mercury veteran Gus Grissom and Roger Chaffee.

1. Who was the only President since Taft to have never made baseball's opening day first pitch while in office?

   a) Bill Clinton
   b) Jimmy Carter
   c) Franklin D. Roosevelt
   d) Richard Nixon

2. For which university did Gerald Ford play football?

   a) Michigan
   b) Notre Dame
   c) Alabama
   d) Texas

3. Which towering president was famed for his intimidation tactic known as "The Treatment"?

   a) Abraham Lincoln
   b) William Howard Taft
   c) George Washington
   d) Lyndon B. Johnson

4. Of what country was former President John Tyler a citizen when he died?

   a) The United States
   b) The Confederate States
   c) Great Britain
   d) France

5. How long did Democrats hold the White House before Republican Ike Eisenhower was elected in 1952?

   a) eight years
   b) 12 years
   c) 16 years
   d) 20 years

1. **Jimmy Carter**

   While Taft threw the very first pitch, Clinton was the first to throw the ball all the way to the catcher from the pitcher's mound.

2. **Michigan**

   After college and prior to WWII, Ford worked as a male model. In 1942 he appeared on the cover of *Cosmopolitan*.

3. **Lyndon B. Johnson**

   The "Johnson Treatment" could last minutes or hours, with the 6-ft. 4-in. Texan only an inch away from touching noses with his target.

4. **The Confederate States**

   Elected to the Confederate House, he died before his term began and was the only President not honored upon his death.

5. **20 years**

   Eisenhower created NASA and the Interstate Highway System— "the largest public works program since the Pyramids."

1. Which World War II battle was called "Hitler's Waterloo"?

   a) Battle of the Bulge
   b) Battle of Midway
   c) Battle of Stalingrad
   d) Battle of France

2. The Civil War Battle of Manassas is also known as what?

   a) Battle of Gettysburg
   b) Battle of Bull Run
   c) Battle of Antietem
   d) Battle of Chancellorsville

3. What president wrote a Pulitzer Prize-winning book while recovering from old war injuries?

   a) George H. W. Bush
   b) Gerald Ford
   c) John F. Kennedy
   d) James Garfield

4. What inspired the name of Vietnam's military defoliant: "Agent Orange"?

   a) its creator: William Orange
   b) color of its storage barrels
   c) the color it turned fields
   d) its primary component: oranges

5. Which war played an instrumental role in the start of the Hatfield and McCoy feud?

   a) Civil War
   b) Revolutionary War
   c) Indian Wars
   d) Spanish-American War

1. Battle of Stalingrad

About 750,000 German soldiers were killed, wounded or missing after the five-month battle. Their forces never recovered.

2. Battle of Bull Run

The first Bull Run was the first major battle of the Civil War. Families went with picnic lunches to watch the fighting.

3. John F. Kennedy

The authorship of *Profiles in Courage* has been debated; speechwriter Ted Sorenson and Kennedy later admitted it was a collaborative effort.

4. color of its storage barrels

The warfare chemical eliminated the food sources for most of the Vietnamese people and caused horrific birth defects.

5. Civil War

Both families were Rebels, except for one McCoy who was murdered. A Hatfield was falsely accused, triggering the feud.

1. What musical featured the lyric "Heil myself! Ev'ry hotsy-totsy Nazi stand and cheer!"?

   a) *The Producers*
   b) *Anchors Aweigh*
   c) *Evita*
   d) *Hello, Dolly!*

2. What future communist dictator had the childhood nickname "Soso"?

   a) Joseph Stalin
   b) Mobutu Sese Seko
   c) Hosni Mubarak
   d) Pol Pot

3. What empire did Hitler consider the First Reich, the predecessor to his Third Reich?

   a) Holy Roman Empire
   b) Weimer Republic
   c) German Empire
   d) Byzantine Empire

4. What U.S. actor has become a thorn in the side of Sudanese dictator, Omar al-Bashir?

   a) George Clooney
   b) Sean Penn
   c) Alec Baldwin
   d) Forest Whitaker

5. The country once run by Mobutu Sese Seko was the setting for which Joseph Conrad novel?

   a) *Heart of Darkness*
   b) *Lord Jim*
   c) *Lord of the Flies*
   d) *1984*

1. *The Producers*

Mel Brooks' beloved Hitler-themed romp won a Tony for best musical, and the original film was voted AFI's 11th best comedy.

2. Joseph Stalin

A young Stalin once asked his mother why she beat him so badly, to which she replied, "That's why you turned out so well."

3. Holy Roman Empire

He considered the German Empire (1871-1918) to be the Second Reich. He denounced Weimer Republic (1918-33).

4. George Clooney

In 2012, Clooney was arrested with his father while protesting at the Sudanese embassy in Washington, D.C.

5. *Heart of Darkness*

The tale of madness was set in the Congo, which became Seko's Zaire; it's now the Democratic Republic of the Congo.

1. What disease blinded Mary Ingalls in *Little House on the Prairie*?

   a) scarlet fever
   b) encephalitis
   c) cholera
   d) diphtheria

2. Lyme disease was named for its place of discovery, a town in what state?

   a) Ohio
   b) West Virginia
   c) Connecticut
   d) New Hampshire

3. Stepping on a rusty nail is most likely to result in which disease?

   a) tularemia
   b) typhus
   c) tetanus
   d) leprosy

4. What fatal infection is often referred to as "rabbit fever"?

   a) diphtheria
   b) gonorrhea
   c) typhus
   d) tularemia

5. What affliction is called the "sacred disease" and has been associated with prophets?

   a) encephalitis
   b) autism
   c) epilepsy
   d) delusions of grandeur

Diseases

Answers

1. scarlet fever

It was the same disease that claimed *Little Women*'s Beth; it also led to the near-burning of *The Velveteen Rabbit*.

2. Connecticut

The tick-borne disease existed for centuries before a 1975 outbreak in Lyme gave doctors a complete understanding.

3. tetanus

John Roebling, designer of the Brooklyn Bridge, contracted the disease after his toes were crushed by a ferry and later amputated.

4. tularemia

It's mostly spread through parasites, but rabbits and humans are also susceptible. It has high potential for biological weaponization.

5. epilepsy

Muhammad, Joan of Arc and Joseph Smith are suspected epileptics; Neil Young, Flo-Jo, Lenin and Caligula were afflicted.

1. In present-day dollar value, which U.S. land purchase was the cheapest, per acre?

   a) Louisiana Purchase, 1803
   b) Gadsden Purchase, 1853
   c) Seward's Folly, 1867
   d) Treaty of Paris, 1898

2. Which President cut taxes the most?

   a) George W. Bush
   b) Ronald Reagan
   c) Richard Nixon
   d) Jimmy Carter

3. What is the all-time best-selling work of American literature?

   a) *The Catcher in the Rye*
   b) *The DaVinci Code*
   c) *Gone with the Wind*
   d) *Charlotte's Web*

4. Reporter Jack White won a Pulitzer Prize for reporting on what President's tax returns?

   a) John F. Kennedy
   b) Richard M. Nixon
   c) Bill Clinton
   d) Ronald Reagan

5. In the 2000s, coinage became bizarrely scarce in which South American country?

   a) Argentina
   b) Brazil
   c) Colombia
   d) Venezuela

1. Seward's Folly, 1867

In 1867, each of Alaska's 375,303,680 acres only cost 2¢ – the Louisiana Territory cost 3¢ per acre.

2. Ronald Reagan

The tax rate was 70% when Reagan took office and 28% when he left. No President before him cut more than 32%.

3. *The DaVinci Code*

Eight non-American books beat it, among them: *A Tale of Two Cities*, *And Then There Were None*, and *The Lord of the Rings*.

4. Richard M. Nixon

His "I'm not a crook" claim was about Watergate and taxes; he took $500,000 deductions for his "vice-presidential papers."

5. Argentina

During the crisis stores gave candy in place of coins when making change, and bus lines sold coins at a profit.

1. Which film led to the moniker "Frat Pack" for a handful of 21st century male comedy stars?

   a) *Zoolander*
   b) *Old School*
   c) *Anchorman*
   d) *Wedding Crashers*

2. Which famed jazz musician went "missing in action" during World War II?

   a) Glenn Miller
   b) Louis Armstrong
   c) Tommy Dorsey
   d) "Count" Basie

3. What soda-maker pulled a commercial featuring Madonna's music video for "Like a Prayer"?

   a) Coca Cola
   b) Pepsi
   c) 7 Up
   d) Dr. Pepper

4. An accused murderer was freed after he was spotted in the background of a scene on:

   a) *Modern Family*
   b) *Mad About You*
   c) *Curb Your Enthusiasm*
   d) *Seinfeld*

5. Which venerable newsman was featured in *Milk*, *Frost/Nixon* and *Apollo 13* via archive footage?

   a) Edward R. Murrow
   b) Tom Brokaw
   c) Walter Cronkite
   d) Chet Huntley

1. *Old School*

"Frat" brothers: Luke and Owen Wilson, Vince Vaughn, Will Ferrell, Ben Stiller, Steve Carrell and Jack Black.

2. Glenn Miller

His plane disappeared while flying between London and Paris. It's speculated he was shot down in friendly fire.

3. Pepsi

It showed burning crosses and other incendiary religious imagery. She still received her $5 million fee even though the commercial didn't air.

4. *Curb Your Enthusiasm*

When the murder occurred, he was at a Dodgers game where the show was coincidentally filming a scene.

5. Walter Cronkite

He applied to NASA after retiring from CBS, hoping to score the "Civilian in Space" spot. The seat was awarded to Christa McAuliffe.

1. What commonplace American toy was first patented in 1866 under the name "bandelore"?

   a) hula hoop
   b) yo-yo
   c) pogo stick
   d) Slinky

2. In what decade did American children first color with Crayola crayons?

   a) 1880s
   b) 1900s
   c) 1930s
   d) 1950s

3. What is broadly considered the world's best-selling toy of all time?

   a) Rubik's Cube
   b) Slinky
   c) yo-yo
   d) Barbie doll

4. Where were Braille, the hypodermic syringe and internal combustion engine invented?

   a) Belgium
   b) Germany
   c) England
   d) France

5. In what decade were American sign language, the stethoscope and bicycle invented?

   a) 1810s
   b) 1780s
   c) 1850s
   d) 1890s

1. **yo-yo**

   The earliest known yo-yos were found in
   ancient Greece and comprised of terra cotta.
   The Greeks' skill at "walking the dog"
   is unknown.

2. **1900s**

   A Yale study found that Crayolas were
   among the top 20 most recognizable scents
   for adults, beating cheese and bleach.

3. **Rubik's Cube**

   It's advertised to have "billions"
   of arrangements but it actually has
   43,252,003,274,489,856,000
   (over 43 quintillion)!

4. **France**

   Napoleon signed the patent for Nicéphore
   Niépce's internal combustion engine.
   Niépce also took the world's first
   photograph in 1822.

5. **1810s**

   Bicycles didn't have pedals until 1838-39.
   Prior to that cyclists just pushed off the
   ground with their feet to gain momentum.

1. The second-largest accidental explosion in history took place in Halifax during what war?

   a) War of 1812
   b) Korean War
   c) World War I
   d) World War II

2. The Dust Bowl was precipitated, in part, because *this* was stripped from the Great Plains?

   a) tumbleweeds
   b) buffalo grass
   c) crab grass
   d) summer wheat

3. In 2009, University of California scientists ranked *what* as the dirtiest coastal ecosystem?

   a) Mississippi Delta, U.S.A.
   b) Sundarbans Delta, Bangladesh
   c) South China Sea, Vietnam
   d) Po River, Venice, Italy

4. The Great Pacific Garbage Patch is mostly comprised of what type of refuse?

   a) chemical sludge
   b) nuclear waste
   c) plastic
   d) discontinued naval vessels

5. In India's 1984 Bhopal disaster over a half-million people were harmed by what?

   a) famine
   b) breached levees
   c) nuclear explosion
   d) gas leak

1. World War I

The SS *Mont-Blanc* was carrying tons of picric acid, TNT, gasoline and guncotton. Two-thousand died and another nine-thousand were injured.

2. buffalo grass

During the Dust Bowl people pickled and ate the plentiful tumbleweeds, along with roadkill when crop growth stopped.

3. Mississippi Delta, U.S.A.

Nutrient runoff from farms along the Mississippi River flow into the delta where they build up with destructive, oxygen-stealing algae.

4. plastic

It is estimated that there's 100 million tons of garbage there, covering more area than the continental United States.

5. gas leak

A pesticide gas leak engulfed the shantytowns that surrounded the plant. An estimated 16,000 people died from it.

Natural Disasters

1. Most of the mammal casualties in Yellowstone's 1988 fires were:

   a) bison
   b) elk
   c) black bears
   d) moose

2. Pan Am Flight 214 crashed in 1963 after lightning struck what part of the plane?

   a) engine
   b) oxygen tank
   c) guidance system
   d) reserve fuel tank

3. One-sixth of Brescia, Italy was leveled in 1769 when lighting struck their store of what?

   a) gasoline
   b) dynamite
   c) gunpowder
   d) cotton

4. *The Little Shop of Horrors* and *The Day of the Triffids* featured what kind of man-eater?

   a) insect
   b) plant
   c) worm
   d) fungus

5. One asteroid deflection tactic involves "painting" it what color to change its trajectory?

   a) white
   b) red
   c) blue
   d) metallic

Natural Disasters

Answers

1. elk

The park had 40,000 total elk. While the 345 casualties exceeded other animal losses, it was less than 1% of the elk population.

2. reserve fuel tank

On average, jetliners in flight are struck by lightning once a year. They're covered in discharge wicks to deflect the bolts.

3. gunpowder

There were 90,000 kilograms of gunpowder stored in the bastion— a literal powder keg. The blast killed 3,000 people.

4. plant

Of the 630 known carnivorous plants, most only eat insects; though some *can* devour rodents.

5. white

"Painting" the asteroid white or black would affect heat absorption, which would, in turn, affect how fast and in what direction it rotates.

1. Who was the only "Mercury Seven" astronaut who didn't pilot a Mercury mission?

   a) Scott Carpenter
   b) Gordon Cooper
   c) Deke Slayton
   d) Wally Schirra

2. Who watched the televised Apollo 11 moon landing from the Oval Office?

   a) Richard Nixon
   b) John F. Kennedy
   c) Lyndon B. Johnson
   d) Gerald Ford

3. Apollo 13's pilot Ken Mattingly was scrubbed when he was suspected of having what ailment?

   a) chickenpox
   b) measles
   c) influenza
   d) strep throat

4. What planet is home to the plateau Aphrodite Terra, which is about the size of Africa?

   a) Earth
   b) Jupiter
   c) Mars
   d) Venus

5. What planet takes approximately 30,800 Earth days to orbit the Sun?

   a) Neptune
   b) Saturn
   c) Uranus
   d) Jupiter

1. Deke Slayton

He was grounded in 1962 due to a heart murmur. He finally went to space in 1975 on an Apollo-Soyuz mission.

2. Richard Nixon

Once Armstrong and Aldrin landed, Nixon spoke to them via telephone-radio transmission from the iconic office.

3. measles

When backup pilot Charlie Duke contracted measles it exposed everyone; Mattingly was expected to get it, but never did.

4. Venus

Venus and Aphrodite are the ancient goddess of love and beauty— Venus was her Roman name, Aphrodite was her Greek name.

5. Uranus

It has 27 known satellites (moons), which are all named for characters from the works of Shakespeare and Alexander Pope.

1. Harry Truman went to bed on election night in 1948 believing what man had beat him?

   a) Dwight D. Eisenhower
   b) Strom Thurmond
   c) Wendell Willkie
   d) Thomas Dewey

2. Born in 1882, in what decade did Franklin Roosevelt become paralyzed?

   a) 1880s
   b) 1890s
   c) 1920s
   d) 1930s

3. Which president made Francis Scott Key's "The Star-Spangled Banner" the national anthem?

   a) John Quincy Adams
   b) Benjamin Harrison
   c) Ulysses S. Grant
   d) Herbert Hoover

4. Calvin Coolidge "exercised" in the White House by riding what?

   a) a stationary bike
   b) a tricycle
   c) an electric horse
   d) a life-size train set

5. Which First Family once had a dog named "Checkers"?

   a) the Nixons
   b) the Kennedys
   c) the Carters
   d) the Reagans

1. **Thomas Dewey**

   Upon returning to D.C. two days after his surprise win, he was handed the Chicago Tribune that inaccurately read: "Dewey defeats Truman."

2. **1920s**

   Some doctors now say that he may have had not polio but Guillian-Barré, which was more likely to hit adults (he was 39).

3. **Herbert Hoover**

   Just three years before Hoover was elected, Francis Scott Key's cousin, F. Scott Fitzgerald, published *The Great Gatsby*.

4. **an electric horse**

   One of silent Cal's favorite pranks was pressing all the desktop buttons that summoned his staff, then hiding while they looked for him.

5. **the Nixons**

   Accused of taking illegal donations, Nixon's defense— the "Checkers Speech"— claimed the dog was the only gift he kept.

1. The United States acquired all but which country at the end of the Spanish-American War?

   a) the Philippines
   b) Guam
   c) Puerto Rico
   d) Indonesia

2. Which country sustained the most casualties in World War II?

   a) Soviet Union
   b) Germany
   c) United States
   d) Japan

3. Which film about the aftermath of World War II costarred a double-amputee WWII veteran?

   a) *Saving Private Ryan*
   b) *The Best Years of Our Lives*
   c) *Sergeant York*
   d) *Schindler's List*

4. In what year did the Berlin Wall fall?

   a) 1979
   b) 1984
   c) 1989
   d) 1994

5. The Battles of Hoke's Run, Cheat Mountain and Poison Spring were all part of what war?

   a) Civil War
   b) War of 1812
   c) Revolutionary War
   d) Mexican-American War

1. **Indonesia**

It was an unpopular treaty— former President Grover Cleveland and Andrew Carnegie petitioned Congress not to approve it.

2. **Soviet Union**

The Soviet Union lost 26.6 million people. More than one third of the Soviet men aged 20-49 were killed in the war.

3. *The Best Years of Our Lives*

Harold Russell got Best Supporting Actor and an honorary Oscar; he's the only actor with two Oscars for one role.

4. **1989**

It fell just two years after Reagan urged Gorbachev to "tear down this wall." The U.S.S.R. collapsed two years after that.

5. **Civil War**

Cheat Mountain was the first battle in which Robert E. Lee led the Confederate army into fighting. The Union won.

1. Who was the first foreign head of state convicted of a crime in a U.S. court?

   a) Saddam Hussein
   b) Osama bin Laden
   c) Manuel Noriega
   d) Ayatollah Khomeini

2. What political group overthrew the Romanov dynasty, ushering in a dictatorship?

   a) Bolsheviks
   b) Social-Democrats
   c) Mensheviks
   d) Prohibitionists

3. What cinematic ballad was Saddam Hussein's campaign theme song in 2002?

   a) "My Heart Will Go On"
   b) "The Way We Were"
   c) "I Will Always Love You"
   d) "Stand By Me"

4. Which despot declared the calendar restarted at Year 0 when he took power in 1975?

   a) Vladimir Lenin
   b) Saddam Hussein
   c) Pol Pot
   d) Mao Zedong

5. Who resigned the Yugoslav presidency shortly after the 1999 NATO bombing of his country?

   a) Enver Hoxha
   b) Nicolae Ceausescu
   c) Slobodan Miloševic
   d) Mikhail Gorbachev

1. Manuel Noriega

Released from a U.S. prison for French extradition in 2010, he was extradited to Panama the next year where he will remain until 2031.

2. Bolsheviks

The Romanovs were murdered a year after being overthrown, becoming martyrs to many; their remains weren't found until 1979.

3. "I Will Always Love You"

He used an Arabic cover version by Syrian pop star Mayyada Bselees and played it in dawn-to-dusk radio broadcasts.

4. Pol Pot

Pol Pot's three-year rule resulted in the deaths of one to three million people, almost a fourth of the country's total population.

5. Slobodan Milošević

He stood trial in the Hague soon after and led his own defense. The trial went on for 5 years; he died in his cell before a verdict was reached.

1. Some of history's most awful epidemics have been caused by this disease, once called "the grip"?

a) syphilis
b) chlamydia
c) influenza
d) cholera

2. What ailment has been called the "royal disease"?

a) epilepsy
b) hemophilia
c) typhoid fever
d) gout

3. What color will a person appear to be if there is excess bilirubin in their blood?

a) yellow
b) blue
c) black
d) gray

4. Which actress' father stopped a near-epidemic of Ebola in Zaire in 1976?

a) Meryl Streep
b) Debra Winger
c) Sally Field
d) Glenn Close

5. Fungus in what grain may have caused the illness that Salemites alleged was "witchcraft"?

a) wheat
b) corn
c) barley
d) rye

1. influenza

There are five animals in which it usually originates: humans, birds, dogs, pigs and horses (however more are susceptible).

2. hemophilia

Queen Victoria was a carrier; she married her children throughout Europe's royal houses where the gene was passed down.

3. yellow

Jaundice is caused by excess bilirubin, indicating stress on, in or near the liver. It's also a symptom of yellow fever.

4. Glenn Close

An American surgeon and pilot, William Taliaferro Close's proactive course of action likely kept Ebola from ravaging the continent.

5. rye

The fungus ergot causes violent fits, choking and hallucinations— all the signs of "bewitching." The drug LSD is an ergot derivative.

1. Which U.S. economic sector has the most employees?

   a) accommodation & food service
   b) health care & social services
   c) retail trade/sales
   d) manufacturing

2. In what state is Tyson Foods based?

   a) Texas
   b) California
   c) Arkansas
   d) Georgia

3. The Carter presidency's economic strife is identified with limited access to what good?

   a) dairy
   b) houses
   c) cars
   d) gasoline

4. How much did the average loaf of bread cost in 1912?

   a) a penny
   b) a nickel
   c) a dime
   d) a quarter

5. Who was a Gilded Age titan of the banking and finance industry?

   a) J.P. Morgan
   b) John D. Rockefeller
   c) Andrew Carnegie
   d) John Jacob Astor

Economy

1. health care & social services

Though the highest-paid careers are in medicine, manufacturing has the highest total payroll of all sectors.

2. Arkansas

It's America's third-poorest state despite being home to the world's largest meat producer, second-largest food company, and Wal-Mart.

3. gasoline

A simultaneous energy crisis and recession caused a gas shortage that left drivers waiting in lines to fill their tanks.

4. a nickel

The average income in 1912 was $1,003, the average house set a family back $4,800, and mailing a letter cost only two cents.

5. J.P. Morgan

Morgan was also the inspiration for "Rich Uncle Pennybags," the iconic character from the Monopoly board game.

1. What rock star was born Farrokh Bomi Bulsara in Zanzibar in 1946?

   a) Freddie Mercury
   b) James Brown
   c) David Bowie
   d) Stevie Wonder

2. What film only won five of Oscar's most coveted awards (a.k.a. "Big Five" Awards)?

   a) *Silence of the Lambs*
   b) *It Happened One Night*
   c) *Gone with the Wind*
   d) *One Flew Over the Cuckoo's Nest*

3. What beloved children's writer penned Johnny Cash's classic poem "A Boy Named Sue"?

   a) Dr. Seuss
   b) Roald Dahl
   c) Shel Silverstein
   d) A. A. Milne

4. Who sent a woman dressed in Indian tribal garb to decline his Best Actor Oscar in 1972?

   a) George C. Scott
   b) Jack Nicholson
   c) John Wayne
   d) Marlon Brando

5. Who started an infamous all-star dance-off during his first and only Oscars hosting gig?

   a) Johnny Carson
   b) Jerry Lewis
   c) David Letterman
   d) Bob Hope

1. Freddie Mercury

He spent much of his youth in India before moving to England. His family were Parsi adherents of Zoroastrianism.

2. *Gone with the Wind*

It received Best Picture, Director, Actress and Screenplay, but Clark Gable lost the Best Actor award to Robert Donat of *Goodbye, Mr. Chips.*

3. Shel Silverstein

Cash heard Silverstein sing it at a party and asked permission to sing it for the San Quentin prison inmates. It was an instant hit.

4. Marlon Brando

It was all a stunt. Ironically, the woman was a Hispanic actress; he still received the award and displayed it proudly.

5. Jerry Lewis

He still claims he made Humphrey Bogart dance with James Cagney at the 1959 Oscars disaster, even though Bogey died in 1957.

1. When and where were roller skates invented?

   a) 1460 in China
   b) 1560 in Germany
   c) 1660 in Scotland
   d) 1760 in Belgium

2. What 15th century invention is often cited as the most important innovation in history?

   a) toothbrush
   b) printing press
   c) pencil
   d) pocket watch

3. In what year did television broadcasts begin in the United States?

   a) 1928
   b) 1938
   c) 1948
   d) 1958

4. The Kelvinator was an early variant of what device?

   a) vacuum cleaner
   b) washing machine
   c) refrigerator
   d) microwave oven

5. What early video game's name was derived from tennis and the Greek prefix for "four"?

   a) *Pong*
   b) *Frogger*
   c) *Megami Tensei*
   d) *Tetris*

Inventions

1. **1760 in Belgium**

   The first roller derby was a nonviolent 3,000-mile marathon in the Chicago Coliseum. Twenty thousand spectators came to watch the event.

2. **printing press**

   Before it, only a few people had access to books, religious texts and political information, as mass communication did not exist.

3. **1928**

   The first broadcasts were merely silhouette images from movies; it was another 20 years before TV's Golden Age began.

4. **refrigerator**

   The Kelvinator was first financed in 1914 by the Buick auto company. Kelvinator later shared factory space with Rolls-Royce.

5. *Tetris*

   It was named for the four segments in a block and the inventor's favorite sport, though the game is nothing like tennis.

Man-Made Disasters
Questions

1. During China's "Great Leap Forward" vast numbers of what bird were killed?

    a) crow
    b) starling
    c) sparrow
    d) hawk

2. What is the primary cause of acid rain?

    a) nuclear waste storage
    b) industrial runoff in rivers
    c) chemical dumping in oceans
    d) burning fossil fuels

3. What body of water was virtually drained by failed attempts to irrigate regional farmland?

    a) Black Sea
    b) Aral Sea
    c) Dead Sea
    d) Red Sea

4. Asia's Vozrozhdeniya Island is nicknamed for what spore-based disease once tested there?

    a) botulism
    b) tetanus
    c) smallpox
    d) anthrax

5. The top three serial killers all came from what South American nation?

    a) Chile
    b) Argentina
    c) Colombia
    d) Brazil

1. **sparrow**

   The Four Pests Campaign also ordered the extermination of rats, flies and mosquitos. Sparrow die-off permitted a locust plague on crops.

2. **burning fossil fuels**

   Emissions mix with clouds, resulting in corrosive precipitation. However, it doesn't melt everything as the name implies.

3. **Aral Sea**

   The lake (between Kazakhstan and Uzbekistan) was sourced for local irrigation and 90% was drained, stranding ships in dirt.

4. **anthrax**

   Abandoned in 1992, "Anthrax Island" was also an open-air testing site for smallpox, bubonic plague and tularemia.

5. **Colombia**

   The three men, who were active from 1969 to the '90s, killed at least 320 total but may have claimed as many as 900 lives.

1. What part of Armageddon is actually safe and scientifically feasible?

   a) space shuttling to an asteroid
   b) drilling 800 ft. of asteroid
   c) landing a ship on an asteroid
   d) blowing up an asteroid

2. Which Moon-bound NASA mission was struck by lightning twice on the launchpad?

   a) Apollo 11
   b) Apollo 12
   c) Apollo 13
   d) Apollo 16

3. What aftereffect of an earthquake leveled 30 city blocks of Anchorage in 1964?

   a) fires
   b) flood
   c) avalanche
   d) landslide

4. Prior to 2000, the costliest tornadoes in U.S. history had victimized which city?

   a) Wichita
   b) St. Louis
   c) Amarillo
   d) Tulsa

5. An 1812 earthquake along what fault line caused the Mighty Mississippi to run backwards?

   a) San Andreas fault line
   b) Ramapo fault line
   c) Humboldt fault line
   d) New Madrid fault line

Natural Disasters
Answers

1. landing a ship on an asteroid

NASA intends for its post-Mars Rover missions to involve landing spacecrafts, and eventually astronauts, on asteroids.

2. Apollo 12

NASA's great jokester, Pete Conrad, the third man on the Moon, exclaimed "Whoopie!" as he took his first lunar step.

3. landslide

The earthquake measured 9.2 on the Richter scale and caused damage in Oregon, California, Hawaii and Japan.

4. St. Louis

An 1896 tornado caused $2.2 billion in damage and killed more than 280 people. The next tornado struck 41 years later and amassed $1.8 billion in damage.

5. New Madrid fault line

In 2012, exactly 200 years later, Hurricane Isaac caused the Mississippi River to run backwards yet again.

1. For what does the astronomical abbreviation "NEO" stand?

   a) nearby extraterrestrial object
   b) nearing Earth overhead
   c) nearing elevatory optimization
   d) near-Earth object

2. What is the largest moon in the Solar System and to what planet does it belong?

   a) Ganymede, Jupiter
   b) Titan, Saturn
   c) Triton, Neptune
   d) the Moon, Earth

3. In what decade was the Big Bang theory born?

   a) 1790s
   b) 1850s
   c) 1920s
   d) 1970s

4. Which spiral galaxy is closest to our own?

   a) Milky Way
   b) Cartwheel Galaxy
   c) Andromeda Galaxy
   d) Centaurus A

5. Mercury and which other planet have no moons?

   a) Venus
   b) Mars
   c) Uranus
   d) Neptune

1. near-Earth object

Most pose no threat to the planet. Those that do are labeled "potentially hazardous objects," or "PHOs."

2. Ganymede, Jupiter

Galileo Galilei is credited with its 1610 discovery. It was named for Zeus' favorite cupbearer of the Greek gods.

3. 1920s

It wasn't named until 1949, when English astronomer Fred Hoyle (who didn't even believe the theory was valid), coined the term on the radio.

4. Andromeda Galaxy

Scientists project that in 3.75 billion years our Milky Way and Andromeda will collide, making one big elliptical galaxy.

5. Venus

The four inner planets only have three moons totals, but the outer planets have (at least) a combined 169 known moons.

1. What position did William Howard Taft hold after the presidency?

   a) Senator from Ohio
   b) Supreme Court Chief Justice
   c) Ambassador to Great Britain
   d) Representative from Ohio

2. Which presidential distinction does Theodore Roosevelt hold?

   a) youngest president
   b) youngest elected president
   c) heaviest president
   d) shortest president

3. Who made Grover Cleveland's two presidential terms non-consecutive?

   a) William McKinley
   b) Chester Arthur
   c) Benjamin Harrison
   d) James Garfield

4. What president, illiterate until marriage, was once an indentured servant and tailor?

   a) Andrew Jackson
   b) Andrew Johnson
   c) Ulysses S. Grant
   d) Abraham Lincoln

5. George Washington's funeral was delayed several days because of his fear of what?

   a) no one coming to his funeral
   b) confined spaces
   c) being buried alive
   d) dirt

1. **Supreme Court Chief Justice**

   Known for his infamous bathtub incident during his miserable presidency, he dropped 100 pounds after leaving office.

2. **youngest president**

   The teddy bear was so named after he refused to "hunt" a bear that was tied to a tree, calling it "unsportsmanlike."

3. **Benjamin Harrison**

   Harrison was the first president to have electricity in the White House, however he wouldn't touch the light switches for fear of being electrocuted.

4. **Andrew Johnson**

   The first president impeached, he spent most of his remaining presidency caring for a family of mice in the Oval Office.

5. **being buried alive**

   He was eulogized by Henry "Light-Horse Harry" Lee as "First in war, first in peace, first in the hearts of his countrymen."

1. What treaty ended World War I?

   a) 1919 Treaty of Paris
   b) Treaty of Versailles
   c) Treaty of Ghent
   d) Treaty of Verdun

2. Which country converted from communism to a republic after the Velvet Revolution?

   a) Czechoslovakia
   b) Hungary
   c) Soviet Union
   d) East Germany

3. Which Confederate general lost an arm after (accidentally) being shot by his own men?

   a) Stonewall Jackson
   b) J. E. B. Stuart
   c) Robert E. Lee
   d) P. G. T. Beauregard

4. What nation was going to be blamed had anything gone wrong during John Glenn's orbit?

   a) Soviet Union
   b) Cuba
   c) East Germany
   d) Japan

5. World War II propaganda posters warned Americans that "Loose Lips" what?

   a) "Take Dips"
   b) "Cause Rips"
   c) "Lose Tips"
   d) "Sink Ships"

1. Treaty of Versailles

The excessive reparations Germany was forced to pay impoverished and embittered the people, ultimately leading to WWII.

2. Czechoslovakia

Also called the "Gentle Revolution," it was unique because it was a nonviolent movement led primarily by student groups.

3. Stonewall Jackson

The arm received its own funeral and gravestone after the amputation. Jackson died and was buried separately a week later.

4. Cuba

"Operation Dirty Trick" was a plot to create evidence showing Cuba harmed Glenn's ship electronically, had he crashed.

5. "Sink Ships"

The phrase warned against discussing military intel and became an enduring idiom, cautioning against indiscrete conversation.

1. *The Communist Manifesto* declared that human history was defined by repeated what?

   a) "class struggles"
   b) "world wars"
   c) "corruption and hatred"
   d) "communist yearnings"

2. The United States would have launched Operation Downfall had which dictator not surrendered?

   a) Joseph Stalin
   b) Benito Mussolini
   c) Adolf Hitler
   d) Hirohito

3. What artist endorsed Joseph Stalin at the end of World War II?

   a) Andy Warhol
   b) Jackson Pollock
   c) Pablo Picasso
   d) Georgia O'Keeffe

4. What U.S. magazine scored a coup in 1994 with a Fidel Castro cover and interview?

   a) *Newsweek*
   b) *Time*
   c) *Cigar Aficionado*
   d) *Vanity Fair*

5. The United Kingdom has compared which dictator's rascist attitude to that of Adolf Hitler?

   a) Islam Karimov
   b) Raul Castro
   c) Hugo Chavez
   d) Robert Mugabe

Dictators
Answers

1. "class struggles"

The 23-page text implored "Workers of the world, unite!" It was another 69 years before the communist movement began.

2. Hirohito

Seven nukes would have fallen on Japan, obliterating the country. Allied ground troops would have followed two days later.

3. Pablo Picasso

In 1950 Picasso received the Stalin Peace Prize from the Soviet government. He remained a loyal communist until he died.

4. *Cigar Aficionado*

The magazine perpetually extolls the virtues of Cuba, on which the United States has a trade and travel embargo.

5. Robert Mugabe

The Zimbabwean president, who ordered 4,000 white farmers to give up their land during a famine, mocked the UK's remark: "I am still the Hitler of my time."

1. Napoleon sold Louisiana after a French army in Haiti was wiped out by slave revolts and:

a) malaria
b) influenza
c) smallpox
d) yellow fever

2. Autism has controversially been linked to what purported cause?

a) head trauma
b) vaccine overload
c) lead-based paint
d) eating meat and dairy

3. Which of the following isn't one of the most likely culprits in a food poisoning outbreak?

a) apples
b) leafy greens
c) potatoes
d) ice cream

4. "Cooties," the modern playground affliction, was also the name for what aggravating disease agent?

a) ringworm
b) tapeworm
c) measles
d) lice

5. Quinine was the first effective treatment for what mosquito-borne disease?

a) yellow fever
b) malaria
c) dengue fever
d) typhus

1. yellow fever

Staying in America was too costly and he needed to fund war with Britain, so he offered the United States a deal they couldn't refuse.

2. vaccine overload

Vaccine-related theories are hotly debated; research linking autism to the MMR vaccine was proved an "elaborate fraud."

3. apples

Mathematician Alan Turing committed suicide by injecting an apple with cyanide, possibly in an attempt to re-enact his favorite fairytale, *Snow White*.

4. lice

Transmitters of disease, lice can reduce life expectancy of their host. They cling to hair with special saliva which makes them very difficult to remove.

5. malaria

Believed to be a major contributor of the fall of the Roman Empire, it also took the lives of Amerigo Vespucci and Vasco de Gama.

1. What is the primary component in the paper used for U.S. currency?

   a) cotton
   b) wood pulp
   c) linen
   d) recycled paper

2. In 2012, who was the richest person in the United States?

   a) Warren Buffett
   b) Bill Gates
   c) Larry Ellison
   d) Charles and David Koch

3. Prior to Bill Clinton, who was the last president to manage four surpluses?

   a) Richard M. Nixon
   b) Ronald Reagan
   c) Lyndon B. Johnson
   d) Harry S. Truman

4. Which state has no sales tax?

   a) Oklahoma
   b) Texas
   c) Delaware
   d) Iowa

5. Who proclaimed that there are only two certainties in life: death and taxes?

   a) Mark Twain
   b) Woody Allen
   c) Benjamin Franklin
   d) Bob Hope

1. cotton

Bills are printed on a durable paper containing three parts cotton to one part linen. In 2010, a bill cost 9.6¢ to make.

2. Bill Gates

Four of the top ten wealthiest were from Wal-Mart's Walton family. New York City mayor Michael Bloomberg was tenth.

3. Harry S. Truman

Under Truman, NATO was created, the U.S. Armed Services was racially integrated, and WWII was brought to a swift end with the first deployed atomic bomb.

4. Delaware

Four other states let consumers shop tax free: Alaska, Montana, New Hampshire and Oregon.

5. Benjamin Franklin

Franklin coined another aphorism about one's finances: "Remember that time is money."

1. Where do Hollywood legends get immortalized in wet cement?

   a) Hollywood Walk of Fame
   b) Grauman's Chinese Theater
   c) Kodak Theater
   d) Sidewalk of Stars

2. In what decade did the iconic "Hollywoodland" sign drop its last four letters?

   a) 1920s
   b) 1930s
   c) 1940s
   d) 1950s

3. Who is the only person with five stars on the Hollywood Walk of Fame?

   a) Walt Disney
   b) Gene Autry
   c) Charlie Chaplin
   d) Clint Eastwood

4. Who got pregnant via affair with Clark Gable, hid out in Europe, then later adopted her own baby?

   a) Ingrid Bergman
   b) Carole Lombard
   c) Vivien Leigh
   d) Loretta Young

5. Where did William Randolph Hearst purportedly murder filmmaker Thomas Ince?

   a) in Hearst's San Simeon mansion
   b) on Hearst's boat
   c) in Ince's convertible
   d) in Hollywood's Roosevelt Hotel

1. Grauman's Chinese Theater

Marilyn Monroe wanted to leave an imprint of her rear and dot her 'i' with a diamond, but was denied both. She dotted her 'i' with a rhinestone instead.

2. 1940s

It was shortened in 1949. The sign is purportedly haunted by the ghost of a starlet who committed suicide there in 1932.

3. Gene Autry

He's the only person to get a star in all five categories: Film, Television, Recording Industry, Radio and Theater.

4. Loretta Young

While the secret was openly known in Hollywood, Judy Lewis didn't learn the truth until her late 20s. Gable never publicly acknowledged her as his daughter.

5. on Hearst's boat

It's rumored that Hearst mistook Ince for Charlie Chaplin, who he suspected of romancing his girlfriend, Marion Davies.

1. Which board game debuted first?

    a) *Monopoly*
    b) *Scrabble*
    c) *Candy Land*
    d) *Clue*

2. Of what material were the first tea bags made in 1908?

    a) paper
    b) cotton
    c) silk
    d) metal mesh

3. According to legend, jazz originated in which city?

    a) Chicago
    b) Paris
    c) New Orleans
    d) New York City

4. Which intellectual luminary was **not** featured in one of Apple's "Think Different" ads?

    a) Thomas Edison
    b) Pablo Picasso
    c) Jim Henson
    d) Steve Jobs

5. In what decade were Prozac, Post-It Notes, the e-mail network and digital watch invented?

    a) 1950s
    b) 1960s
    c) 1970s
    d) 1980s

Inventions

1. ***Monopoly***

   The British Secret Service made a version
   of Monopoly with maps, compasses, escape
   tools and real money for POWs being held
   by the Nazis.

2. **silk**

   Cold tea bags are often used medicinally, as
   a treatment for sunburn and snowblindness.

3. **New Orleans**

   Louis Armstrong, Mahalia Jackson, Jelly
   Roll Morton and Fats Domino were all part
   of the New Orleans jazz scene.

4. **Steve Jobs**

   Jobs was never featured, though his Apple
   creations earned him a place among
   America's pantheon of great inventors.

5. **1970s**

   A 3M chemist created the adhesive on
   Post-Its five years before he could talk
   anyone into applying it to a product.

1. Agent Orange destroyed more than 25 million acres of what country?

   a) Vietnam
   b) Korea
   c) Japan
   d) Soviet Union

2. Hurricane Katrina was worsened considerably when what was breached?

   a) flood walls
   b) levees
   c) canals
   d) dams

3. At what kind of event were 169 people killed in an infamous 1944 tent fire in Hartford, Connecticut?

   a) wedding
   b) high school graduation
   c) circus
   d) church revival

4. How many days were the 52 American hostages in Iran held?

   a) 100 days
   b) 444 days
   c) 666 days
   d) 999 days

5. In 1875 what city in the British Isles was flooded with whiskey that later caught on fire?

   a) Dublin
   b) London
   c) Edinburgh
   d) Liverpool

1. Vietnam

The United States wanted to corral the people into major cities to better control them; 1.5 million flooded into Saigon ghettos.

2. levees

It was ultimately the costliest U.S. natural disaster ($81 billion) and the third-deadliest Atlantic hurricane in U.S. history.

3. circus

The Ringling Brothers Barnum & Bailey tent was coated in paraffin and gasoline, making it a fireball waiting to happen.

4. 444 days

The Ayatollah despised Jimmy Carter. They released the hostages minutes after Ronald Reagan was sworn into office.

5. Dublin

Over 500,000 liters flooded the streets and caused a series of explosions, scorching three city blocks. Four people died trying to drink the flaming booze.

1. In 2012, Hurricane Sandy pulled what iconic amusement park feature into the ocean?

a) Ferris wheel
b) merry-go-round
c) roller coaster
d) food stands

2. The north lake on Poás Volcano has a pH of zero thanks to an overabundance ot what chemical?

a) sulfuric acid
b) hydrochloric acid
c) benzoic acid
d) hydrogen chloride

3. Pyroclastic flows threaten nearby people and property during what kind of disaster?

a) blizzard
b) monsoon
c) mudslide
d) volcanic eruption

4. The ongoing armed conflicts in Sudan, Syria and Afghanistan were preceded by what crisis?

a) flood
b) plagues of insects
c) drought
d) earthquake

5. Who helped avert untold deaths by discovering the miracle antibiotic, penicillin?

a) Jonas Salk
b) Louis Pasteur
c) Edgar Crookshank
d) Alexander Fleming

Natural Disasters

Answers

1. roller coaster

Sandy pulled the "Star Jet" off the wooded boardwalk of Seaside Heights, New Jersey, leaving it partially submerged.

2. sulfuric acid

To compare, lemon juice has a far less acidic pH (2). Poás' south lake is clear and surrounded by a cloud forest.

3. volcanic eruption

Water can't cool a pyroclastic flow. Its heat causes the water to evaporate, which in turn propels it to flow faster.

4. drought

Local militias, like Sudan's Janjaweed and the Afghans' Taliban, are often organized as a result of droughts and famines.

5. Alexander Fleming

He was a notorious slob and made the find accidentally on a dirty lab dish. Penicillin heals syphilis, scarlet fever and diphtheria, among many others.

1. What meteor shower is most spectacular in August (from Earth's point of view)?

   a) Andromedid meteor shower
   b) Perseid meteor shower
   c) Pegasid meteor shower
   d) Radiant meteor shower

2. What is split into two sections by the Cassini Division?

   a) Solar System
   b) Milky Way
   c) Saturn's rings
   d) Asteroid Belt

3. What is the smallest planet in our Solar System?

   a) Venus
   b) Mars
   c) Pluto
   d) Mercury

4. Approximately how far away from Earth is the Hubble Telescope?

   a) 75 miles
   b) 350 miles
   c) 5,000 miles
   d) 106,500 miles

5. What moves 1.5 inches further away from the Earth each year?

   a) Moon
   b) Sun
   c) Mars
   d) Halley's Comet

Planets and Stars

Answers

1. Perseid meteor shower

The Perseids are associated with the Swift-Tuttle comet. Their peak visibility is between August 9-14 every year.

2. Saturn's rings

Of the many gaps in Saturn's rings, the 3,000-mile Cassini Division, which appears near the middle, is the most obvious.

3. Mercury

Mercury's 88-day orbit of the Sun is the most erratic (least perfectly circular) orbit of all eight planets.

4. 350 miles

Its mirror was initially flawed— it was 2.2 micrometers "off" (a width seven times narrower than a strand of hair).

5. Moon

It's moving at roughly the same speed at which our fingernails grow. As a result, Earth's rotation gradually slows.

1. "Dark horse" President Polk cheered Manifest Destiny, acquiring Oregon under the slogan:

   a) "Westward, ho!"
   b) "54-40 or fight!"
   c) "Tippecanoe and Tyler, too!"
   d) "Free Soil-Free Job-Free Men"

2. Martin Van Buren was the hero of a street gang, the "Van Buren Boys," on what sitcom?

   a) *Friends*
   b) *The Big Bang Theory*
   c) *Cheers*
   d) *Seinfeld*

3. After a "miserable" presidency, John Quincy Adams represented what state in Congress?

   a) Virginia
   b) Massachusetts
   c) Pennsylvania
   d) New York

4. James Monroe's presidency was known by what name?

   a) "Gilded Age"
   b) "Manifest Destiny"
   c) "Era of Good Feelings"
   d) "Gay Nineties"

5. James Madison was the "Father" of what founding charter?

   a) Articles of Confederation
   b) Virginia Declaration of Rights
   c) Constitution
   d) Declaration of Independence

1. **"54-40 or fight!"**

   Polk was invoked in Franklin Pierce's campaign slogan: "We Polked you in '44, We shall Pierce you in '52."

2. ***Seinfeld***

   He was nicknamed after his hometown, "OK" (for Old Kinderhook), as well as "the Little Magician" for his adept political skill.

3. **Massachusetts**

   "Old Man Eloquent" condemned slavery for 17 years, even after the topic was banned. He died after collapsing in the House of Representatives.

4. **"Era of Good Feelings"**

   He crossed the Delaware with Washington during the Revolutionary War and was re-elected unanimously, save for one vote.

5. **Constitution**

   He was one of the authors of *The Federalist Papers* promoting the Constitution. He also authored the Bill of Rights.

1. In what war did Theodore Roosevelt lead a scrappy military band known as the Rough Riders?

   a) World War I
   b) Mexican-American War
   c) Spanish-American War
   d) Civil War

2. What Southern city refused to celebrate the Fourth of July from 1863-1945?

   a) Gettysburg, PA
   b) Manassas, VA
   c) Atlanta, GA
   d) Vicksburg, MS

3. What was the first American war to employ lotteries to raise war funds?

   a) World War I
   b) Civil War
   c) War of 1812
   d) Revolutionary War

4. Whose popular sauce originated after Union soldiers burned all but one of his crops?

   a) Heinz's ketchup
   b) McIlhenny's Tabasco sauce
   c) French's yellow mustard
   d) Hellmann's mayonnaise

5. The Battles of Amiens, the Isonzo, and Verdun were all part of what war?

   a) World War I
   b) World War II
   c) The Hundred Years' War
   d) The Easter Rising

1. Spanish-American War

Their name was borrowed from the show "Buffalo Bill's Wild West and Congress of Rough Riders of the World."

2. Vicksburg, MS

After Robert E. Lee lost at Vicksburg on July 4, 1863, the city refused to celebrate the holiday until the end of WWII.

3. Revolutionary War

In the Civil War the first income tax was levied in the Union to fund the war; later wars were funded by raising taxes.

4. McIlhenny's Tabasco sauce

Popular During a 1932 "Buy British" campaign, Tabasco was removed from Parliament's dining hall, igniting a "Tabasco Tempest."

5. World War I

Amiens ended trench warfare on the Western front; the first day was popularly referred to as "the black day of the German Army."

1. What was the first major social reform Mikhail Gorbachev attempted in the Soviet Union?

   a) expelling gay Soviets
   b) integrating schools
   c) curbing alcohol abuse
   d) fighting obesity

2. Who has been called the "French Stalin" for masterminding the Reign of Terror?

   a) Cardinal Richelieu
   b) Charles De Gaulle
   c) Maximilien Robespierre
   d) Napoleon

3. Hitler's favorite dessert was what French pastry, the name of which means "lightning"?

   a) strudel
   b) Linzer torte
   c) éclair
   d) baklava

4. In what American fast food chain did Tiananmen Square student protestors meet?

   a) Kentucky Fried Chicken
   b) McDonalds
   c) Taco Bell
   d) Subway

5. Traces of what chemical were found in forensic tests on Napoleon's hair?

   a) mercury
   b) estrogen
   c) arsenic
   d) sulfur

1. curbing alcohol abuse

His plan included raising the price on alcohol, which ultimately cost the country an estimated 100 billion rubles.

2. Maximilien Robespierre

He was ultimately sentenced to death. He tried to shoot himself, missed, and went to the guillotine without a lower jaw.

3. éclair

The notorious sweet tooth was always on a sugar high— he put seven teaspoons of sugar in his coffee, and even added it to his wine.

4. Kentucky Fried Chicken

The Tiananmen Square's KFC stands 3 stories tall and is the word's largest. Students met there to plan their movement against Deng Xiaoping.

5. arsenic

His hair had 100 times the average amount of arsenic. It was a popular poison in his time because it was undetectable.

1. What is the most frequently consumed addictive drug in the United States?

   a) nicotine
   b) alcohol
   c) caffeine
   d) cannabis

2. The 11th and 12th Presidents, James Polk and Zachary Taylor, were both killed by what?

   a) tuberculosis
   b) cholera
   c) heart disease
   d) pneumonia

3. George Washington required his soldiers to get inoculated against what disease?

   a) measles
   b) bubonic plague
   c) smallpox
   d) scarlet fever

4. The annual *Jerry Lewis Telethon* held on Labor Day was held to raise funds to combat what?

   a) HIV/AIDS
   b) multiple sclerosis
   c) muscular dystrophy
   d) cancer

5. After skin cancer, what is the most common type of cancer in the United States?

   a) breast cancer
   b) prostate cancer
   c) colorectal cancer
   d) lung cancer

Diseases
Answers

1. caffeine

An overdose is highly unlikely – an adult would have to consume the same amount of caffeine that's in 80-100 cups of coffee.

2. cholera

A 1991 exhumation of President Taylor's remains revealed cholera or gastroenteritis to be the cause of death.

3. smallpox

He considered it one of his best strategic moves of the war; his own pre-war bout with smallpox likely left him sterile.

4. muscular dystrophy

From 1966-2009 the telethon raised almost $2.5 billion. 2010 marked the first year Jerry Lewis did not serve as host.

5. lung cancer

It is the most commonly diagnosed cancer in the world, and subsequently has the highest mortality rate.

1. Whose presidency averaged the highest top tax rate in U.S. history?

   a) John F. Kennedy
   b) Bill Clinton
   c) Jimmy Carter
   d) Dwight D. Eisenhower

2. Which U.S. Vice President resigned when he was charged with tax evasion?

   a) Dan Quayle
   b) Spiro Agnew
   c) Nelson Rockefeller
   d) Hubert Humphrey

3. Which Founding Father was the very first Secretary of the Treasury?

   a) James Monroe
   b) Thomas Jefferson
   c) Alexander Hamilton
   d) James Madison

4. The first time the federal government collected income tax, they did so to fund what?

   a) Civil War
   b) Revolutionary War
   c) World War II
   d) Transcontinental Railroad

5. According to a 2001 study, which day of the week is the worst for the U.S. stock market?

   a) Friday
   b) Monday
   c) Wednesday
   d) Tuesday

1. Dwight D. Eisenhower

Ike's top rate never dipped below 91%. He used the revenue to build the Interstate Highway System and create NASA.

2. Spiro Agnew

Gerald Ford was appointed to replace him. Ford then assumed the presidency eight months later when Nixon resigned.

3. Alexander Hamilton

He was a staunch Federalist; he created the first National Bank and had the federal government pay the states' war debt.

4. Civil War

The Union collected the first income tax in 1861; it was the primary reason why they were better equipped to win the war.

5. Monday

Even the stock market hates Monday. Wednesday is the market's best day and most consistent. Friday is the most volatile.

1. Which Hollywood bombshell's boyfriend was stabbed to death by the actress' own 14-year-old daughter?

   a) Rita Hayworth
   b) Ava Gardner
   c) Lana Turner
   d) Betty Grable

2. How did Dr. Sam Sheppard, immortalized in *The Fugitive*, spend his later working life?

   a) retired as a doctor
   b) he never found work
   c) became a pro wrestler
   d) became an ice cream man

3. What music icon's dream to create a *Harry Potter* musical was dashed by J.K. Rowling?

   a) Madonna
   b) Paul McCartney
   c) Michael Jackson
   d) Andrew Lloyd Webber

4. Who couldn't make the Vulcan salute, requiring the *Star Trek* crew to tape his fingers?

   a) William Shatner
   b) Leonard Nimoy
   c) Zachary Quinto
   d) Chris Pine

5. What politico picked a fight with Murphy Brown to his own detriment?

   a) Ronald Reagan
   b) Richard Nixon
   c) Dan Quayle
   d) Bill Clinton

Hollywood
Answers

1. Lana Turner

Cheryl Crane stabbed Johnny Stompanato, who was abusing Turner. Crane was never convicted on grounds of self defense.

2. became a pro wrestler

After his 1966 acquittal during a retrial, he wrestled under the name "The Killer" until his death in 1970.

3. Michael Jackson

The Vatican's former chief exorcist once decried yoga, saying, "It leads to evil— just like reading *Harry Potter*."

4. William Shatner

Nimoy started the hand gesture, basing it on an Orthodox Jewish ritual his grandfather did known as "Blessing Hands."

5. Dan Quayle

At the end of the episode addressing the single-mother debacle, Murphy left a truckload of potatoes on Quayle's driveway.

1. For what purpose was Play-Doh originally invented in the 1930s?

   a) to clean wallpaper
   b) as a modeling compound
   c) as a baking ingredient
   d) as a home repair compound

2. What fabric, composed of coal, air, and water, was invented in 1938?

   a) polyester
   b) nylon
   c) chiffon
   d) gabardine

3. Metal shortages during what war caused women to forsake corsets for newfangled brassieres?

   a) Spanish-American War
   b) Civil War
   c) World War I
   d) World War II

4. Frisbee-like flying discs were first sold on California beaches in 1937 as "Flyin'" what?

   a) "Tin Saucers"
   b) "Pie Plates"
   c) "Garbage Can Lids"
   d) "Cake Pans"

5. Who is the only U.S. President to acquire a patent for an invention?

   a) James Garfield
   b) Thomas Jefferson
   c) Abraham Lincoln
   d) Theodore Roosevelt

Inventions

1. to clean wallpaper

It wasn't repackaged as a children's modeling compound until 1955; over the next 50 years, two billion cans were sold.

2. nylon

It proved invaluable with World War II on the horizon— nylon was used in parachutes, tires, tents, ponchos and rope.

3. World War I

According to female activist Betty Friedan, "bra burning" was a myth; however, many women did stop shaving their legs and wearing make-up.

4. "Cake Pans"

The first one was sold by 17-year-old Fred Morrison when a guy offered him a quarter for a five-cent pan he was tossing on the beach.

5. Abraham Lincoln

His 1849 patent was for an apparatus that lifted boats over shoals so they wouldn't get stuck on banks in shallow water.

1. What became U.S. law the day after the Boston Molasses Flood of 1919?

   a) women' suffrage
   b) Prohibition
   c) "separate but equal"
   d) Pure Food and Drug Act

2. London's East End was flooded by 1.2 million liters of what potent drink in 1814?

   a) whiskey
   b) beer
   c) gin
   d) scotch

3. The Bee Gees' "Have You Seen My Wife, Mr. Jones" tells of what kind of disaster?

   a) nuclear disaster
   b) shipwreck
   c) plane crash
   d) mining disaster

4. What NASA mission was memorialized with the Latin phrase: "Ad astra per aspera"?

   a) Apollo 1
   b) Space Shuttle Challenger
   c) Apollo 13
   d) Space Shuttle Columbia

5. Over what state did the German Hindenburg airship disaster occur, killing 36 people?

   a) New York
   b) New Jersey
   c) Florida
   d) Ohio

Man-Made Disasters
Answers

1. Prohibition

Coincidentally, most of the molasses was for alcohol production. Modern-day Bostonians say they can still smell molasses on hot days.

2. beer

A 20-foot-high vat burst, setting off a chain reaction. Eight people drowned while one allegedly died from alcohol poisoning.

3. mining disaster

Titled "New York Mining Disaster 1941," it's usually called by its aforementioned subtitle. It was their first hit.

4. Apollo 1

The phrase means "a rough road leads to the stars." A launchpad fire during a routine test claimed the lives of three astronauts.

5. New Jersey

While it's the best-known airship calamity, twice more people died 4 years earlier when the *USS Akron* exploded off the coast of New Jersey.

1. One of the biggest explosions in history was the 1908 impact of a meteor in which country?

   a) Russia
   b) United States
   c) India
   d) Australia

2. What asteroid was once feared to be on 2029 and 2036 collision courses with Earth?

   a) Hypnos
   b) Icarus
   c) Apophis
   d) Orpheus

3. Which 20th century eruption triggered a 13-mile landslide— one of the largest in history?

   a) Mount Pelée, Martinique
   b) Nevado del Ruiz, Colombia
   c) Mount St. Helens, U.S.A.
   d) Santa María, Guatemala

4. What natural disaster is measured and categorized "zero" thru "five" by the Fujita Scale?

   a) hurricane
   b) heat wave
   c) earthquake
   d) tornado

5. What disaster is measured and categorized on a 1-5 range by the Saffir-Simpson Scale?

   a) earthquake
   b) hurricane
   c) tornado
   d) blizzard

1. Russia

The blast flattened 80 million trees and was 1,000 times more powerful than the atomic bomb detonation at Hiroshima.

2. Apophis

Scientists now know it won't hit us in 2029, nor will it pass through the "keyhole" that would send it back to hit us in 2036.

3. Mount St. Helens, U.S.A.

Its lahars, or volcanic mudslides, traveled as far as 50 miles to the Columbia River. Ash spread as far as 285 miles.

4. tornado

Of the fifty-eight F5 or EF5 tornadoes on record, twenty-fve hit Kansas, Iowa, Oklahoma and Texas – oddly, Ohio has been hit by four.

5. hurricane

Altogether, Category 5 Atlantic hurricanes – Katrina, Wilma, Rita ('05), Andrew ('92) and Ivan ('04) – have caused $199 billion of ruin.

1. How many stars are within one light year of Earth?

   a) one star
   b) one-hundred stars
   c) millions of stars
   d) none

2. Which planet's equator rotates at a different speed than its poles?

   a) Saturn
   b) Neptune
   c) Venus
   d) Mercury

3. Which astronomical body is also called a "planetoid" or "minor planet"?

   a) asteroid
   b) comet
   c) meteor
   d) moon

4. Some Inuit believed that if you whistled at this, it would come down and cut off your head:

   a) Moon
   b) Aurora Borealis
   c) Halley's Comet
   d) meteor showers

5. The "Pillars of Creation" are part of what type of celestial body?

   a) galaxy
   b) comet
   c) nebula
   d) star

Planets and Stars

Answers

1. one star

Our Sun is the only star anywhere near Earth. The next closest star, Alpha Centauri, is 4.37 light years away.

2. Neptune

Since it's made mostly of gas, the poles rotate in about 12 Earth hours while the equator finishes in about 16 hours.

3. asteroid

The largest known asteroid, Ceres, is 950 km wide. By comparison Pluto is 2,306 km wide while the Moon is 3,474 km wide.

4. Aurora Borealis

Other Inuit people believed the radiant lights depicted their deceased family members dancing in the next life.

5. nebula

Hubble Space Telescope's image of the Eagle Nebula's star formations (the Pillars) is arguably its most famous image.

1. What presidential romance is legendary, revealed in the letters of the "dearest friends"?

   a) John & Abigail Adams
   b) Franklin & Eleanor Roosevelt
   c) Abraham & Mary Todd Lincoln
   d) George & Martha Washington

2. What guest refused to stay in the Lincoln Bedroom again after seeing Honest Abe's ghost?

   a) Queen Elizabeth II
   b) Charles De Gaulle
   c) Queen Victoria
   d) Winston Churchill

3. Who sent his son the election day note: "Don't buy a single vote more than is necessary"?

   a) Theodore Roosevelt
   b) Joseph P. Kennedy
   c) Sr.   William Arthur
   d) George H. W. Bush

4. Which modern wonder did Chester Arthur and Grover Cleveland dedicate on its opening day?

   a) Lincoln Memorial
   b) Empire State Building
   c) Brooklyn Bridge
   d) Jefferson Memorial

5. Who was the first President elected after women's right to vote was recognized in 1920?

   a) Woodrow Wilson
   b) Calvin Coolidge
   c) William Howard Taft
   d) Warren G. Harding

1. John & Abigail Adams

At least 1,100 letters still exist, all addressed to "My Dearest Friend," though he also called her "Miss Adorable."

2. Winston Churchill

One night in 1942 his ghost knocked on the guest room door of the Dutch Queen Wilhelmina, who fainted upon seeing him.

3. Joseph P. Kennedy

JFK joked about it on election night, saying Joseph proclaimed, "I'll be damned if I'm going to pay for a landslide!"

4. Brooklyn Bridge

Arthur was then the President; Cleveland was the governor of New York. He succeeded Arthur as President two years later.

5. Warren G. Harding

He was the first to campaign with Hollywood friends; he was shown in newsreels with Douglas Fairbanks and Mary Pickford.

1. Where did General George Armstrong Custer make his "Last Stand"?

   a) Wounded Knee
   b) Killdeer Mountain
   c) Little Bighorn
   d) Crazy Snake

2. Who was the Persian Gulf War's equivalent to "Tokyo Rose"?

   a) "Baghdad Betty"
   b) "Karbala Katie"
   c) "Tehran Tammy"
   d) "Amman Annie"

3. What spy proclaimed: "I only regret that I have but one life to lose for my country"?

   a) Mata Hari
   b) T. E. Lawrence
   c) Patrick Henry
   d) Nathan Hale

4. Which was **not** among the first foods rationed during World War II?

   a) bacon
   b) butter
   c) chocolate
   d) sugar

5. Which candymaker created the chocolatey D ration bar given to soldiers in World War II?

   a) Hershey's
   b) Bosco
   c) Whitman's
   d) Tootsie Roll

1. Little Bighorn

He was a noted Civil War vet who fought at Bull Run, Antietam, Gettysburg and was present when Lee surrendered to Grant.

2. "Baghdad Betty"

She reportedly warned G.I.s that their wives were dating Bart Simpson. The statement was later verified to be a Johnny Carson joke.

3. Nathan Hale

He was only 21 when the British captured and hanged him, prompting his infamous declaration on the gallows.

4. chocolate

Petrol was the first good rationed (September 1939). The following January, bacon, butter, and sugar were rationed.

5. Hershey's

The army asked that it only taste "a little better than a boiled potato" so G.I.s wouldn't eat them unless they needed to.

1. What dictator attempted to give Nation of Islam leader Louis Farrakhan over $1 billion?

   a) Saddam Hussein
   b) Ayatollah Khomeini
   c) Muammar Gaddafi
   d) Osama bin Laden

2. What dictator was cited in the Beatles' "Revolution"?

   a) Mao Zedong
   b) Leonid Brezhnev
   c) Pol Pot
   d) Ayatollah Khomeini

3. On what beach were Hitler's forces strongest during their otherwise failed D-Day defense?

   a) Pointe du Hoc
   b) Utah Beach
   c) Sword Beach
   d) Omaha Beach

4. Idi Amin lived out the rest of his days in what country?

   a) Iraq
   b) Saudi Arabia
   c) Iran
   d) Libya

5. How did the Ayatollah Khomeini disrupt his own funeral in 1989?

   a) sat up due to rigor mortis
   b) he fell out of his casket
   c) exploded
   d) talking

1. **Muammar Gaddafi**

   The Clinton administration blocked the gift legally; nonetheless Farrakhan received an estimated $8 million over the years.

2. **Mao Zedong**

   John Lennon wrote the song during the aftermath of the United States' disastrous 1968 Tet Offensive in Vietnam.

3. **Omaha Beach**

   Omar Bradley considered giving up but the Allies prevailed by scaling the bluffs. One in 10 invading Allies died there.

4. **Saudi Arabia**

   He claimed to be a devout Muslim in order to receive sanctuary. The Saudi royals paid him a vast annuity to stay out of politics.

5. **he fell out of his casket**

   When his wood casket broke open spectators grasped at him to obtain relics. For his second funeral he was placed in a secured steel coffin.

1. In the Middle Ages people with what disease were forced to carry rattles?

   a) bubonic plague
   b) smallpox
   c) scabies
   d) leprosy

2. In the 1990s scientists learned what circus animal could transmit tuberculosis to people?

   a) lions
   b) chimpanzees
   c) elephants
   d) giraffes

3. Which internal organ is the most severely damaged by dysentery?

   a) kidneys
   b) intestines
   c) liver
   d) stomach

4. In what country was "Typhoid Mary," one of the first asymptomatic carriers, quarantined?

   a) United States
   b) England
   c) Ireland
   d) Germany

5. Which contamination disease claimed the lives of Abigail Adams, Wilbur Wright and Stephen Douglas?

   a) cholera
   b) dysentery
   c) typhoid fever
   d) diphtheria

1. leprosy

They were often confined to leper colonies,
preferably on islands; however, we
now know that the disease is not easily
contagious.

2. elephants

Circuses aren't the only locale of concern:
eight workers at a Tennessee elephant
sanctuary contracted TB in 2009.

3. intestines

Francis Drake died from dysentery. He was
buried at sea in full armor and a lead coffin,
which divers have never found.

4. United States

The turn-of-the-century cook spent about
27 years confined to NY's North Brother
Island after infecting dozens of people.

5. typhoid fever

Louisa May Alcott, Georgia O'Keefe
and Frank McCourt are among the many
victims who contracted and beat the illness.

1. In what year could Americans e-file their tax returns for the first time?
   a) 1985
   b) 1995
   c) 2005
   d) 2010

2. At its sales peak in 1985, what children's playmate was its own half-billion-dollar market?
   a) Cabbage Patch Kid
   b) Barbie
   c) G.I. Joe
   d) Tickle Me Elmo

3. What was the federal minimum wage in 1960?
   a) 50¢ an hour
   b) $1 an hour
   c) $2.50 an hour
   d) $5.00 an hour

4. What member of Bill Clinton's 1992 campaign exclaimed: "It's the economy, stupid!"
   a) George Stephanopoulos
   b) James Carville
   c) Hillary Clinton
   d) Bill Clinton

5. The all-time lowest U.S. income tax rate was what percentage, in effect from 1913-16?
   a) 1%
   b) 5%
   c) 10%
   d) 20%

1. **1995**

   Computers revolutionized complex tax preparation; e-filing and P.C. programs have been slowly phasing out tax accountants.

2. **Cabbage Patch Kid**

   They inspired the first toyshop stampedes; Elmo's frenzy was the most violent and led to $1,500 black market pricetags.

3. **$1 an hour**

   Adjusted for inflation, 1968's wage of $1.60 was the highest ever, while 2012's wage of $7.25 is among the lowest.

4. **James Carville**

   He brought it back 20 years later, coauthoring *It's the Middle Class, Stupid!* with Clinton advisor, Stan Greenburg.

5. **1%**

   The top rate during that time was only 7%. The rate for low-income citizens didn't reach the double digits until WWII.

1. A cover of what beloved Beatles' tune was the theme song for *The Wonder Years*?

   a) "A Hard Day's Night"
   b) "All You Need Is Love"
   c) "With a Little Help from My Friends"
   d) "Hey Jude"

2. What "faith" was cited by enough Brits in the 2001 census that the country recognized it?

   a) Muggle
   b) Wizard
   c) Jedi
   d) Hobbit

3. Jason Schwartzman, Talia Shire and Nicholas Cage are all part of what Hollywood family?

   a) the Fonda family
   b) the Douglas family
   c) the Coppola family
   d) the De Laurentiis family

4. What "Sexiest Man Alive" staged his own abduction on a 2002 episode of *Jackass*?

   a) Brad Pitt
   b) Matt Damon
   c) Channing Tatum
   d) George Clooney

5. In 1987 who became the first woman inducted to the Rock and Roll Hall of Fame?

   a) Janis Joplin
   b) Aretha Franklin
   c) Tina Turner
   d) Diana Ross

1. "With a Little Help from My Friends"

At 13, Fred Savage became the youngest person ever nominated for an Outstanding Lead Actor Emmy (in comedy or drama).

2. Jedi

The U.S. Department of Defense also recognizes it now, allowing military personnel to have it stamped on their dogtags.

3. the Coppola family

Talia is Francis Ford Coppola's sister; Schwartzman is her son; Cage is the son of their brother August.

4. Brad Pitt

Plucked off a sidewalk and thrown in a van, it prompted bystanders to call the police. The authorities weren't amused.

5. Aretha Franklin

Some of the Queen of Soul's best hits were covers – "Respect" was Otis Redding's and "A Natural Woman" was Carole King's.

1. Which Old Hollywood actress patented the technology for Bluetooth and Wi-Fi in 1942?

   a) Katharine Hepburn
   b) Hedy Lamarr
   c) Bette Davis
   d) Claudette Colbert

2. What kitchen tool won the highest prize at the 1893 World's Fair in Chicago?

   a) electric microwave
   b) electric blender
   c) electric dishwasher
   d) electric toaster

3. The inventor of the gasoline-powered automobile founded what car company?

   a) BMW
   b) Mercedes-Benz
   c) Maybach
   d) Porsche

4. In which country did the first bicycle, motorcycle and automobile rides take place?

   a) United States
   b) Germany
   c) England
   d) France

5. In what century were carbonated drinks, the guillotine and manned hot-air balloons created?

   a) 1600s
   b) 1700s
   c) 1800s
   d) 1900s

1. **Hedy Lamarr**

   No one believed her "frequency hopping" was even viable for 20 years; it's now the basis of modern telecommunication.

2. **electric dishwasher**

   It was also the debut of the original Ferris wheel and a memorable demonstration in which Nikola Tesla shot lightning from his fingers.

3. **Mercedes-Benz**

   The first gasoline pumps were created in 1885, not to fuel cars, but to provide fuel for kerosene lamps and stoves.

4. **Germany**

   In 1949 the ground stability of jet engines was tested by strapping one to a motorbike. It reached a speed of 70 mph.

5. **1700s**

   Ironically, King Louis XVI helped improve the design of the guillotine, unaware at the time that he and his wife, Marie Antoinette, would later be beheaded with it.

1. The Great Chicago Fire of 1871 was popularly believed to have been started by what animal?

   a) horse
   b) pig
   c) cat
   d) cow

2. In what country did 26 swarms of Africanized killer bees escape from a lab in 1956?

   a) United States
   b) Brazil
   c) Morocco
   d) United Kingdom

3. The radiation leakage of Chernobyl was how many times worse than the Three Mile Island disaster?

   a) 5 times worse
   b) 10 times worse
   c) 30 times worse
   d) 55 times worse

4. The Oklahoma City Bombing occurred exactly two years after what other act of terror?

   a) Ruby Ridge
   b) Branch Davidian siege
   c) '93 World Trade Center bombing
   d) last Unabomber attack

5. In 1980, Congress created *what* as a moneyed trust to clean up hazardous materials?

   a) FEMA
   b) Superfund
   c) EPA
   d) Conservations Corps

1. cow

A hack journalist made up the cow story. A man named "Pegleg" Sullivan is now believed to have ignited the blaze.

2. Brazil

They reached the United States by 1990; while they're more aggressive and attack-prone, their stings are no more potent.

3. 55 times worse

Almost 100% of the gases in Chernobyl's reactors were released and 33 people died as a result. No one died at Three Mile Island.

4. Branch Davidian siege

The bombers were motivated by what they saw as government mishandling of the Branch Davidian and Ruby Ridge events.

5. Superfund

It allows the EPA to urge responsible parties to clean sites they've contaminated, otherwise Superfund covers the cleanup costs.

Natural Disasters

1. What volcano's 1883 eruption had 13,000 times the force of the Hiroshima bomb?

    a) Krakatoa
    b) Vesuvius
    c) Mount Tambora
    d) Mount St. Helens

2. A fearsome "supervolcano" is churning under what U.S. national park?

    a) Yosemite
    b) Crater Lake
    c) Yellowstone
    d) Hot Springs

3. What state was most affected by the 1980 Mount St. Helens eruption?

    a) Oregon
    b) Washington
    c) Montana
    d) Wyoming

4. From what Massachusetts town did *The Perfect Storm*'s Andrea Gail set sail?

    a) Boston
    b) Martha's Vineyard
    c) Gloucester
    d) Cape Cod

5. Survivors of the 2010 Haiti earthquake faced an outbreak of what, due to dirty water?

    a) dysentery
    b) cholera
    c) typhoid fever
    d) hepatitis

1. Krakatoa

It was felt as much as 3,000 miles away and caused blood red sunsets, inspiring Munch's iconic painting *The Scream*.

2. Yellowstone

If it erupted in the near future, it's estimated that ash would reach as far as 2,000 miles, polluting vegetation and country's water supply in its wake.

3. Washington

For two months prior to the eruption, tremors and steam vents shook the state, an indication that an the event was imminent.

4. Gloucester

In 1713, the first schooner was built there. Over the years, this fisherman city has lost over 10,000 men to the sea.

5. cholera

It was ironically introduced by aid workers. By the end of the year, cholera had claimed 3,333 lives – nearly 50 a day.

1. Which large planet did the spacecraft Galileo orbit before crashing into its surface?

    a) Mars
    b) Saturn
    c) Jupiter
    d) Venus

2. Which planet is home to Olympus Mons, the highest mountain in our Solar System?

    a) Mercury
    b) Jupiter
    c) Neptune
    d) Mars

3. Which noted American author "came in" and "went out" with Halley's Comet?

    a) Ernest Hemingway
    b) Walt Whitman
    c) Mark Twain
    d) Tennessee Williams

4. Which planet has a large white storm patch named "Scooter"?

    a) Jupiter
    b) Mars
    c) Uranus
    d) Neptune

5. What astronomer was fond of saying we are "star stuff, contemplating the stars"?

    a) Carl Sagan
    b) Neil deGrasse Tyson
    c) Brian Cox
    d) Isaac Asimov

1. Jupiter

Launched by Space Shuttle Atlantis, Galileo reached its Jovian destination with the help of Earth and Venus' gravity.

2. Mars

It's a 14-mile tall shield volcano – it's the second-tallest mountain on any world known to man.

3. Mark Twain

Born 14 days after its 1835 pass, he said not following it out would be a tragedy. He died one day after its 1910 return.

4. Neptune

Scooter is one of three visible Neptunian storms. The others appear very deep blue: the "Great" and "Small" Dark Spots.

5. Carl Sagan

In the '50s, the Air Force tasked him with figuring out how a dust cloud would expand in space if we nuked the Moon.

1. Who did John Dean claim was the only person who outranked him on Nixon's "Enemies List"?

   a) Bob Woodward
   b) Gerald Ford
   c) "Deep Throat"
   d) Ted Kennedy

2. Which pre-Civil War President still had living grandchildren as of 2012?

   a) Millard Fillmore
   b) Zachary Taylor
   c) John Tyler
   d) James Buchanan

3. Which President saw the people whittle away his 1,400-pound wheel of cheese in two hours?

   a) Andrew Jackson
   b) Thomas Jefferson
   c) Abraham Lincoln
   d) Franklin D. Roosevelt

4. What mosquito-borne ailment was afflicting First Lady Lucretia Garfield when her husband was shot?

   a) yellow fever
   b) malaria
   c) encephalitis
   d) smallpox

5. Which 19th century President sent a diplomat to Russia named Cassius Clay?

   a) James Buchanan
   b) Rutherford B. Hayes
   c) John Tyler
   d) Abraham Lincoln

1. "Deep Throat"

Dean was the former counselor who revealed the list existed. Nixon died in 1994 never knowing Deep Throat's identity.

2. John Tyler

He was 63 when his 13th child (of 15) was born; Lyon Tyler had two sons in the 1920s, when he was in his 70s.

3. Andrew Jackson

He didn't want to drag the "evil-smelling horror" back to Tennessee at the end of his term; 10,000 people took a piece.

4. malaria

She was recovering in New Jersey. She raced to his side; her train went so fast it broke a piston and nearly derailed.

5. Abraham Lincoln

A Kentuckian (like Lincoln and the other Cassius Clay) he refused to take the role of major general unless Lincoln signed an emancipation proclamation.

1. Joan of Arc played a pivotal role in which war?

   a) Seven Years' War
   b) Hundred Years' War
   c) War of the Roses
   d) the Crusades

2. What is the longest running war in American history?

   a) Vietnam War
   b) War in Afghanistan
   c) Revolutionary War
   d) Iraq War

3. Which World War II battle was the most deadly engagement in U.S. history?

   a) Battle of Iwo Jima
   b) Battle of France
   c) Battle of the Bulge
   d) Battle of the Rhineland

4. How many days after the end of the Civil War was Abraham Lincoln assassinated?

   a) 5 days
   b) 14 days
   c) 30 days
   d) 60 days

5. The Battles of Rotterdam, Dunkirk and the Bulge were all part of what war?

   a) World War I
   b) World War II
   c) The Hundred Years' War
   d) The German Revolution

1. Hundred Years' War

DNA tests on a jar of remains originally believed to be Joan's, showed that a rib bone actually belonged to an Egyptian mummy.

2. Vietnam War

Around 58,000 U.S. soldiers lost their lives and 100,000 were left critically disabled. The average age of soldiers who were killed: 23 years.

3. Battle of the Bulge

It was America's largest and bloodiest battle fought on the Western front during WWII, with 89,500 casualties.

4. five days

He is considered by some to be the last casualty of the war, since his death occurred so close to the South's surrender.

5. World War II

Rotterdam was a German win in the Netherlands; the Bulge was a bloodiest battle on the Western Front, and a German loss.